Align and Bloom

**How to Dig into the Soil of Your Soul,
Clear the Blockages for Growth,
and Bloom into Your Authentic Self**

Brittany Rose

Get instant access to the
Align and Bloom workbook and
guided meditations by scanning
the QR code or visiting
web address listed below.

www.phasesofgrowth.org/align-and-bloom

To all spiritual seekers,
may you always find the light.

Planting Seeds

Seeds are first buried
deep in the earth's darkness.
They must crack open
to find their way to the light.
Through growth you find
your authentic self.
It's time to align and bloom.

Introduction

The Tools for Growth

Throughout your lifetime, you go through many different *phases of growth*, repeatedly stepping into darkness, only to work your way back to the light. Each time discovering a deeper layer of your being, illuminating, healing, and transforming the aspects of who you are. It is this way for all people, but most especially seekers. Seekers are people on a lifelong quest for authenticity, joy, peace, and most importantly, Love.

To grow flowers, first you need to prepare by gathering your tools and nurturing the soil. That is what the first section of this book is about—the tools I use to dig into the soil of my soul and uncover blockages for growth.

Every person, at their core, is a beautiful spiritual being of Love. Yet living in the physical world, we are also multifaceted. People are kind and they are hurtful. People are brave and they are frightened, both confident and self-conscious. We are in a constant ebb and flow between states of being, fluctuating between various thought patterns and emotional experiences.

If you are unaware of the parts of yourself that are guiding this ebb and flow, then you can get stuck in pain and anger, or in fear and doubt. Therefore, I want to help you learn how to heal the blocks to your consciousness and become aware. This book will also teach you how to

1

open to spiritual guidance and the natural flow of Love. When you live with this kind of openness, then you are aligned with your most authentic self and are more likely to experience a peaceful life.

I keep talking about Love, and yes, the capitalization is intentional. What do I mean? Love is the highest vibration in the Universe. It is an all-encompassing energy field of creation. Love, to me, is God, Spirit, the Universe, All-That-Is. We are born of Love, we come from Love, our most basic essence is divine Love. Opening to Love supports healing and alignment with your soul's highest path, purpose, and potential.

On earth, change is constant. You are in a state of flux from the time you enter the earth until you leave. Each round we enter a new phase of growth, spiraling through connections and deeper understandings of the human experience.

When you are learning a lesson, whether for the first, or the fifth time, you are digging deeper into that spiritual assignment, and that is wonderful. Your path is perfect. Your journey is always meant for your highest good. There are, however, ways of making this life more comfortable. This requires an examination of your unhealed parts, bringing them to the light, and then planting new seeds to grow into a healthier bloom.

Reconnecting to Love

A few years ago, I felt like I was solidly on a path becoming aligned with my authentic self. And then, life happened. I left my husband of seventeen years— exactly half my life at that point—and moved in with my grandmother, also becoming her caregiver. I joined a fitness community (Diamond Dallas Page Yoga or DDPY) and found a group of people who made me feel like I belonged. I believe that divine guidance led me to DDPY to get healthy and find my soul-mate. In the course of two years, I got divorced, moved three times— the last one to a new state, changed jobs and became a hospice social worker for the first time. Oh, and I also lost over one hundred pounds.

My physical existence transformed in every way possible, and for a myriad of reasons, distance grew between myself and my spiritual connection. I focused so much of my time and energy on the physical that I felt like I had much less room for my inner world.

In the second half of this book, I will do something most people would not dream of. I will let you read my journal chronicling a month of my path to living an energy conscious and spiritually guided life. It is the story of how I dig deep into my being to uncover the parts of me that need healing. I am sharing it with you to give you an idea of how to apply the lessons in the first section into your own healing journey.

My goal is to help you become your most authentic, loving, creative, spiritual self. In a previous part of my life, I had been wide open to my spiritual energy. It guided many of my actions and led me places I never would have imagined.

However, numerous monumental transitions led me to having a dysregulated nervous system. Becoming a hospice social worker really sent my anxious parts over the edge. I stopped many of my spiritual and mental health practices because I simply did not feel like I had enough time. I see now this was an excuse a parts used to protect me. In reality, what I'd done was prioritize other things.

Since January of 2023, I've been adjusting to a new life in Virginia, a new living situation, and new experiences. New is not bad, but all the new can get overwhelming at times. At the end of a long day, I just wanted to turn my mind off and decompress. But because of the state of my mental health when I started writing this, I was reminded that doing my spiritual practices is just as necessary as food and water.

Although I may sometimes feel overwhelmed by all the changes in my life, there is always time to practice wellness and open to Spirit. This connection helps me deal with the stress, and somewhere along the way I forgot this truth. I don't have to over complicate it, I can simply take a breath and ask: *Divine energy please pour into me, heal me, open and align me to Love.*

I just did this, in fact, while writing these words, and I could feel energy humming through my body, changing my vibration to one of peace. Try it out, using my words or your own, and see if you notice a shift in your being.

That's what we are going for, shifts to embody a greater wholeness. To work with our authentic selves and the Universe to release the blockages, fears, and aspects of our lives that are not aligned with our greatest good.

The Universe wants you to learn and grow, but it also wants you to embrace and be in the energy of Love. Love is the most powerful force of the Universe. Love is the answer to all questions. You are in the vibration of Love when you are being curious, compassionate, and creative. Love is the energy present when your soul is alight with joy. It is also there when you are practicing gratitude and just simply being in the moment. Love surrounds you. The truth is, your essence is Love.

My goal is to get back to being open and aligned with Love. Being in this state allows our most beautiful and authentic light to shine. When we are in this vibration, we are blooming. I was there for a while, and I know I can get there again. It is quite possible that the first six months of 2023, I went through these trials and unsettling periods of time in part so I could write this book. I had to fall down again so I could document how I got myself back up.

I wrote parts of the first section in 2020, when I was in a vastly different place in my life. My spirituality was the most important thing to me and, most likely, kept me alive, because I was so physically unhealthy and clinically depressed. I have revised and edited the first section, but reviewing what I wrote in the past was a beneficial reminder of all the practices I have at my disposal.

Get a journal out and prepare yourself to go inside and reflect. This is a guide to help you explore your inner world. It can be scary, so go at a pace that feels comfortable for you. I encourage you to do this work in conjunction with a trained mental health professional if that is the level of support you need. I know from my own experience and the clients I've worked with, the more you can connect with your internal system, the better you're able to heal. But sometimes, we need a companion to hold our hand and gently guide us on our path.

First, we'll go into the darkness, then we *align and bloom.*

Journal Prompts

All the journal prompts are also found in your Align and Bloom

Workbook, which you can download by going to: https://www.phas esofgrowth.org/align-and-bloom

In your workbook or journal write, draw, or in some other manner express in whatever way feels right for you, the answers to these questions. Do not filter yourself! Allow yourself to be open and express whatever wants to come through.

In what ways do you want to grow?

What has blocked your growth?

What are some phases of growth you've already experienced? Lessons learned?

What helped you integrate these lessons?

Awareness

You must feel to heal.

For some, looking inside can be a terrifying experience. The body's inner world does not always feel like a safe place for those who have experienced significant trauma. It is common for people to spend much of their free time numbing to ignore, or escape, their feelings. We numb ourselves through alcohol, drugs, binge eating, over-exercising, distraction, or chronically staying busy. When a person's internal landscape is perpetually dysregulated, they look for an escape.

I love food. For many years, I numbed by binge eating. Being overly full created a buffer between me and intense emotions. The fuller I was, the less emotional gravity I felt. I have worked incredibly hard, and continue to do so, to develop a healthy relationship with eating and exercise. For most of the last two years, I was solid in this endeavor. I mean, I lost over one hundred pounds by eating whole nutritious foods and exercising daily. But lately, I have noticed small steps backwards towards old unhealthy eating habits. I know part of my journey will be to meet this head on and explore what is going on there.

Being able to go inside the chaos of the internal world and look at the different emotions being expressed is a way of getting to know our system at a deeper level. The more in tune we are with ourselves, the easier we can release unaligned aspects of our lives and transform.

It takes acclimating yourself to the idea of going inside your mental headspace and exploring. To live an authentically aligned life, it helps to get comfortable with quiet and stillness. I recommend that you make space in your schedule for purposeful reflection. It's valuable to learn how to tolerate experiencing your emotions so that they can process through your system and release. Being present with yourself isn't always easy, but it's worth it!

Understanding Energy

We are all made up of moving energy in the form of atoms, molecules, and electrons. The basis of our existence is energy in motion. Quantum physics tells us that matter and energy are the same, connected by invisible threads. To walk, talk, eat, or even think, we use energy to complete these tasks. Think of your body like an electrical circuit. We all have an amazing ability to work with electromagnetic, electrical, and subtle energies to improve our health and wellness.

How your emotions and thoughts vibrate in your energetic field determines the overall quality of your physical health. There is evidence that shows perceived stress influences an individual's immune response and the inflammation levels in that person's body. Inflammation is associated with most major diseases. Stress can create disruptions in the flow of subtle energies in and around the body. When energy is out of balance and not flowing smoothly the body is more likely to manifest illness.[1]

Throughout human history many cultures and spiritual traditions have talked about an energy that gives life to all: an energy with consciousness. People in the East refer to it as qi, chi, or in yoga they refer to it as prana. I am trained in Reiki, which is a Japanese modality of energy balancing and rejuvenation. Reiki refers to "Universal Life Force Energy." The word is comprised of two parts- rei, meaning spiritual wisdom, and ki, meaning life force energy. This definition acknowledges the spiritual consciousness that is connected to and forges all that is in our reality.[2] This energy that so many refer to, using different words, I think of as Love. It is the divine creator that exists in everything and everyone.

7

You are comprised of multiple subtle energy systems, a few examples of which include your auric field, your chakras, and your meridians. Science refers to them as the subtle energy systems of the body because they have yet to come up with ways to measure them[3]. The energy of your aura and chakras are vibrating at a frequency that is undetectable by most human eyes and brains. Even though most of us cannot see these energy systems, they are very important, and have a huge impact on the quality of our health and lives.

There are those who refer to emotions as energy in motion. Feeling and processing emotions is critical not only for mental health, but for a person's physical health as well. Preventing yourself from feeling only forces the emotional energy to get trapped within you, creating blockages. Some experiences are too painful, scary, or impactful and they get stuck, unable to complete their cycle. The body holds onto stress and trauma if it cannot fully process the experience through the nervous and energy systems. Unprocessed or stuck emotional energy can develop into disease.

These are not just "woo-woo" thoughts about how energy connects with the body. One study between trauma and its effects on overall health later in life documents the dire consequences of growing up in a fight, flight, or freeze environment. In 1995, the CDC-Kaiser Permanente Adverse Childhood Experiences (ACE) Study observed the connection between childhood trauma and later physical health issues. The study showed that experiencing childhood trauma had a high correlation between adult illnesses such as heart diseases, cancer, bone diseases, and many other physical health challenges later in life.[4]

Often, during a traumatic event, the experiencer cannot process the survival response through their nervous system fully, and so there it sits waiting. An example of this is the aftermath of a car accident—hours later sometimes the body will shake, get cold, tense up, and begin hurting. This is the nervous system releasing all the energy it stored up from the accident, because it had to be in survival mode. But once the system recognizes that it's safe, it allows the processing to go forth. The stored fight-or-flight energy from the nervous system needs to be released, and it can manifest in some unusual ways. It might be through shaking, burping, yawning or some other physiological process.

The first time I remember it happening to me was when I had a stressful interaction with a family I was doing therapy with. Because of safety issues, the police had to be called. I came home from work and was trying to relax and suddenly I started shaking uncontrollably. Luckily, I had learned about nervous system release and allowed myself to breathe through it. Had I not known what was happening I may have panicked and made things worse for myself.

The nervous system can usually release easily when it's an isolated instance of stress. However, what if a trauma happens, and it's just one of many? What if the nervous system can no longer recognize safety because it never feels safe? If someone cannot create stability in their environment, then traumatic energy gets stuck and remains unprocessed. It will not just exist there though—it will pop up at inopportune times. It can make a person hypervigilant, unable to relax, have nightmares, experience flashbacks, and view the world through a dark lens.

This is how your nervous system adapts to protect you. Unfortunately, the result is keeping you stuck in terror.

Embodied Mindfulness

Through increased awareness you gain increased consciousness. Your body is constantly speaking to you—but you must choose to listen. The nervous system sends clues about what's happening as physiological sensations. These sensations correlate with the energy balance of our system. By tuning in, a person can recognize the connection with bodily sensations and emotional experiences. For instance: heart racing, heavy breathing, and muscle tension may indicate someone is experiencing fear or anger. A heaviness in the body, pain, and feeling the urge to cry might signal sadness.

Everyone's emotional states manifest differently, so it's important to get connected with your body and start paying attention. Often your sensations will clue you into your emotional state before your mind recognizes what is going on. Once you realize that your body is tight you can take a deep breath and release the tension. When you understand what your body is communicating you can respond to it with care. If you notice anxiety before it gets out of control then you are better able to manage it, and the more likely the episode will be shorter and less intense than if you unconsciously allow yourself to spiral. Sensations can help you figure out how to best respond to the external world's input.

For some, looking inwards is extremely uncomfortable. Learning how to numb emotions and your sensations may have served as a way of protecting you from trauma, dysfunction, and instability growing up. While this is understandable, being dissociated from your emotions makes it difficult to fully live. How can you embrace all of life's joys and challenging lessons if you're not present, or if you're only half aware of the experience? We are meant to experience life and all its richness. Our lives are scrap quilts made of many colors and dimensions, woven together with our internal experiences. We need to learn how to be with ourselves to fully understand, heal, and grow.

Tuning into your body is helpful to get acquainted with the subtle energies. When you're mindfully aware, you can sense changes in vibrations, depending on the situation. This can help you discern whether something is aligned with your highest good. You can use this to investigate the alignment of people in your life, a circumstance you find yourself in, or a purchase you want to make. Tune in to your body and notice what you sense. You can start simply, by setting an intention to be open to feeling the subtle energies. If something feels tense, dark, or heavy, this could indicate that it's something you don't want to engage with. If, on the other side, it feels light, airy or easy, then this is a vibration that matches your highest good. Pay attention to how things make you feel, both emotionally and physically.

There are many methods of tuning into yourself. Yoga practices are an excellent way to bring mindful awareness to your breathing and your body, through stretching and holding different poses. I love to connect with my body lovingly. Personally, I might practice mindful awareness while I put lotion on my skin or give myself a massage.

The following exercise is a beneficial practice and will help you become accustomed to paying attention to your body and noticing its diverse sensations. Recordings of all the guided meditations can be found at: www.phasesofgrowth.org/align-and-bloom

· · ·

Body Scan Exercise

Take a few deep breaths to center yourself and set the intention to be mindfully aware of your body for the next few minutes. Ask your mind to just notice without judgment what your body feels like.

Begin at your right foot, noticing the sensations in your foot, how it feels touching the floor, in your sock, or in your shoe. Observe the sensations you feel inside your foot itself. Pay attention to the temperature of your foot. Just notice and become aware.

Next, bring this same level of mindfulness to your left foot for a few moments, noticing and observing it.

Continue moving your awareness up your body systematically one body part at a time; noticing the sensations in your right calf, left calf, each of your thighs, stomach, chest, one arm then the other, all the way until you get to the top of your head.

Sit in the quiet for a few more moments, noticing your entire body.

Repeat this exercise often to develop a connection with your body and its method of communication.

There is a saying that I think is valid: Listen to the whispers of your body before you hear its screams. Befriend your body, notice what feels good and what doesn't without judgment. With this new intimacy you can make conscious decisions and align with physical and emotional wellness.

Thoughts+Emotions+Behaviors=Vibration

Everything is energy, both the tangible and the intangible. Thoughts and feelings resonate at different vibrational frequencies. Processing emotional experiences is important for mental wellness. To do this one must first become aware of their limiting beliefs and the energy imprint these thoughts have.

If I say to myself frequently words like, *I'm stupid, I'm an idiot, I'm so dumb,* well naturally I am going to believe these things about myself. In traditional Cognitive-Behavioral Therapy (CBT), a therapist would say, "How does thinking these things make you feel?" and you'd say, *Geez, well not so great. I feel pretty sad and angry at myself.* And then the well-trained therapist would ask you, "What do these negative thoughts and emotions make you do?" After thinking about it for a moment you'd probably answer, *I don't put myself out there, I didn't go to college, I never try for new jobs or promotions, I stay in my lane of what I feel I can accomplish.* This example shows how a person's negative thoughts about themselves influence their feelings, which directs how they interact with the world.

While clinical therapists have been helping people understand the connection between their thoughts, feelings, and behaviors for some time, there is a very important missing component from this conversation. These things added together determine your *vibration*. Your vibration is fluid and always changing, but the essence of your frequency is how the Universe knows what to bring into your experience. Stick yourself on the fridge because you're a magnet!

The attention you give your thoughts, feelings, and actions determines what you will receive. If you often think, "I am poor," and talk about scarcity in your life, your energy will align with poverty, and this will remain true for you. The Universe does not discriminate or punish. It is simply responding to the frequency that you emit.

These concepts refer to the Law of Attraction; it is a universal law that is understood by many. You have to radiate the quality and emotions of the energy you want to bring into your life. Gratitude is a powerful point of attraction. When you express gratitude, the Universe understands that this is something you appreciate and want more of and so it will help align your experiences to bring more of that into your life.

If you complain a lot, if you worry a lot, if you think about worst-case scenarios over and over in your head, this will become a part of your frequency and you will create more of these experiences in your life. The Universe will literally give you something to complain about—not to be cruel, but because it responds to vibration.

People often have a difficult time with this concept, especially when they have experienced hardships. Understanding the Law of Attraction is not about assigning blame. It is about becoming empowered and living the life you want.

Shame is an enormous block for progress and growth. No one feels good thinking they are responsible for the terrible things that have happened in their life. Assigning blame and feeding into shame just keeps people stuck. Instead, use your heartache and challenges to expand your understanding with compassion and heal.

You are not at fault for what happened for you in the past. I say "for you" because each experience assists your growth. Looking at challenges as opportunities creates a paradigm shift out of victim mentality. It helped me to see how everything happens for my benefit, even the difficult experiences. Some lessons are more painfully learned than others. But gratitude and elevating perspectives helps you integrate your lessons with ease.

You can empower yourself for a smoother existence from now on by matching your vibration with all the good that you wish to bring into your life. The Universe will give you what you give your attention to—energy flows where attention goes. Make sure your vibration is flowing towards what you want instead of what you don't want.

Another important thing to realize is that your point of attraction is in the present moment. This is one reason mindful awareness is so important. You can only decide your magnetic frequency in the here and now. You already broadcasted in the past and have yet to do so in the future. When you notice your energy shifting to a vibration of sadness, anger, or other lower vibrational frequencies you get to make conscious choices about what you want to do.

Some days you may need to be with emotions longer than others because it's not always easy to shift into a higher vibration. All of this is normal. Do not judge yourself for where you are on your journey. Allow what needs to be to just be. It is so important that you accept yourself. You are doing the best you can. As you walk through life you learn, heal, and experience. Because of this, your 'best' improves. And when you can shift from a less pleasant emotion, do it, no matter how small of step it is towards a better feeling frequency.

What is the story you tell yourself about you, your life, your relationships, the world? Energetically speaking, the words we speak internally and externally have an enormous impact on our realities. Therefore, it is very important to pay attention to your thoughts. What are the messages that your brain sends to you regularly? What are the internalized belief systems that influence the way you feel and behave?

Do you believe you're destined to be mediocre? Or do you think you can accomplish your goals?

Because our thoughts influence our feelings, which influences our behaviors and vibration, it is critical to not only become emotionally aware but also more cognizant of the running commentary that constantly goes through your brain. Now is it truly possible to be aware of all your thoughts? No, we would all go crazy if that were the case. But you can start with some purposeful time to reflect and observe your stream of consciousness.

Go inwards and start noticing. Don't judge what you discover, just greet it with open curiosity. We will talk about ways of rewiring any unaligned belief systems throughout the book. Right now, I just want you to notice. Write down what you observe in a journal or somewhere else so you can come back to it later.

The Cycle of Emotions

There are those who engage in what I consider "toxic positivity" and label it spiritual. Everything must be sunshine and roses, and if you do not always feel completely positive then bad things are going to happen. However, life is more complicated and so are our reactions to our experiences. It is not realistic, or healthy, to never allow yourself to feel angry or sad. Denying these emotions can make people feel ashamed when they have these very natural feelings. We are born to learn from life, which means our experiences are meant to be complex, and multifaceted.

Of course, part of the journey of life is to figure out how to follow your heart's song, how to pursue your soul's passion and gifts, how to connect with others, how to love ourselves and the world. On this journey you will not only experience happiness, but you will also experience sadness, loneliness, and great Love. And from your joys and heartaches, most importantly, you will learn from it all. If we only lived in Love and harmony, there would be no expansion or growth. Your spirit incarnated in the earth realm because there is a spectrum of emotions and experiences, all of which help with conscious expansion.

Instead of trying to avoid anything negative, it is better to feel your feelings without dwelling on them or trying to push them away. Notice what the feelings are like inside your mind and body. It is necessary to allow the cycle of emotional energy to complete itself, like a wave that we can ride as it rises and falls. By engaging in mindful practices, it is easier to do this without dwelling on the issue, or avoidance. This is truly *being* with our experiences. It is not always easy, but as with anything, it becomes more natural over time.

I encourage people to sit with their emotions for as long as they need to, or for as long as they can tolerate them. Give your feelings a name to help create some separation from them. Instead of saying "I am angry", like anger is your identity, try saying, "I am feeling angry." A shift of one word can change the whole vibration, and help you detach from the emotional energy.

Do not attempt to jump from depths of despair to pure joy, as those emotional energies are too far apart on the vibrational spectrum. However, something like entering a state of neutrality or acceptance may be an easier path to navigate from sadness initially.

If you're going to learn how to befriend your system, start by getting into the practice of asking yourself, *what do I need?* And then, tune in for the answer. It might be an inner knowing or a thought that crosses your mind telling you to breathe, stretch, drink some water, or ground your energy.

As you become more mindful, you may notice more discomfort in your body. This is normal and will continue to help you meet all of your experiences, pleasant and otherwise. If you notice stress or tension, one thing you can do is imagine breath coming into the part of your body, your lower back for example, and then on your exhale release the stress and tension through the breath from that same area.

Burnout: The Secret to Unlocking the Stress Cycle, a book by Emily Nagoski, Ph.D. and Amelia Nagoski, D.M.A is phenomenal, and I highly recommend reading it. One thing that stuck with me from the book is the practice of bringing mindful awareness to crying. Instead of letting yourself be consumed by the emotional experience of crying, you notice the sensations in your body, the tears in your eyes, rolling down your face, how your breathing shifts while you are crying. Doing this helps to create a sense of separation between yourself and the emotion, allowing you to shift into the mindful observer. When your focus is on being observant than the emotion itself, you can process through the stress cycle more easily.[5]

Another beneficial way of helping to process stuck energy is through movement. It can be as simple as taking a short walk or stretching. Movement helps the body and nervous system regulate, which can bring you back to a place of harmony.

Becoming more mindfully aware, to me, is the first step towards creating alignment in your life. To successfully work through your challenges, there first needs to be a non-judgmental recognition of their presence. From there, you can learn how to make conscious choices to alter your thoughts, feelings, behaviors, and ultimately, your energy.

Journal Prompts

How present am I in my daily life?

What prevents me from being more present?

What are some things I can do to increase my mindful awareness or my sensations, emotions, and thoughts?

Parts of Self

Exploring the Complexity Within

You are a multidimensional being. This means that you exist in many layers. Think of yourself like an onion (maybe a less pungent one). Part of the work you need to do is peel back those layers until you get to the core self, the spiritual self. Though you are here in the physical world where you have your five senses, as we have been discussing, there is so much more to the world energetically than what is experienced by those senses. There are different levels of consciousness that we can access through our channel of light, which is our connection to Spirit.

Personality Parts

Internal Family Systems (IFS), created by Dick Schwartz, posits that we all have different parts of self, or different aspects of the ego.[6] Think of when you're experiencing an internal battle such as, "part of me feels like eating a gallon of ice cream" and "part of me wants to be healthy and eat only nutritious foods". These two parts exist in the same person, yet they have their own distinct wants and motivations. Okay, yes, those parts exist within me! They developed out of my experiences growing up, belief systems I embodied, and coping behaviors I turned to for comfort.

When you are unconscious of a part and their fears and motivations, you may lead a reactive life. Taking life as it comes rather than being a co-creator of your own reality. Your personality parts will do whatever it takes to keep you safe, and unfortunately, they can get aggressive if they think it will protect you. Sometimes they are extremely negative to make you feel uncomfortable and submit to their safety measures.

These protective parts are your ego. Ego is fear-based and a survivor. It sees the world through a very narrow lens where resources are scarce, and that the world is a dangerous and lonely place. Ego believes you are separate from others, and it has to fight for your survival. Often your parts bully you into staying in your safe little bubble. But inside the bubble is no way to live and you are reading this book to pop, or at the very least expand, that bubble.

Although its approach is often not the best, your ego really is trying to help. It is important to meet your parts with compassion and openness, to hear them out to gain, and gain a greater understanding of their purpose in your system. I try to not get angry with my fear-based protective parts or view them as bad. These parts serve a purpose, regardless of how misguided it is. Often they are communicating a need that you must address. Once I am aware of the part's purpose, I can release the limiting emotional and energetic patterns. Through this, I align with the vibration of my authentic self.

Authentic Self

In IFS, there is also what the model calls *self energy*. I think of self energy as my most authentic and spiritual self. Some people call it their higher self. The authentic self's essence is Love. It is the truth of us, and the wisest part of our beings. Healing can be done with parts of self and spiritual energy through going inwards, exploring, releasing blocks to Love, and transforming your emotional and energetic system.

We will discuss the authentic self in much more detail in the next chapter. But for now, I wanted to introduce the idea to you. Your parts are aspects of your ego and personality, your authentic self is your spirit.

I was doing IFS work with myself before I knew what IFS was, through the spiritual practices of illuminating my shadows and working with my higher self to heal. While you can do this work alone, I recommend that for traumatic experiences, or ones where you feel stuck, that you work with a trained mental health professional. Sometimes we need another person to be present and hold space for us to let our parts know it is safe to let go.

Communicating with Parts

As a therapist I teach people how to separate from and talk with their parts. To do this, I might say, "The part of me that wants to eat a gallon of ice cream, please step forward and separate so I can talk to you. Tell me what's going on?" and then I get quiet and listen. It will amaze you how quickly you hear your part respond once you figure out how to separate it from the rest of your system. I might hear (or just have an inner knowing of) my ice cream loving part say, "I'm stressed, and I know it will make me feel better." Having this information and knowing that I am not actually craving ice cream at all but craving to feel better allows me to me to think about my choices. I have the opportunity to choose a healthier way to cope, or sometimes I just accept that part's desires and eat some ice cream but not the entire gallon—all things in moderation, my friends.

Awareness of what is behind your thoughts and behavioral patterns allows you to choose how to respond to emotional triggers. The more you get to know your parts the easier it is to do this. First, you need to learn how to create separation in your system. This comes with learning how to go inside, notice your sensations, and breathe into this part of your body, asking for the part to separate. If I am trying to work with a specific anxiety part, for example, I would ask for the part to step forward and separate from me. Then I look inside and notice where I felt the part in or around my body and breathe into that space to encourage it to separate. You'll notice that you're separated from your parts when you can view the part's energy without being consumed by it. You're the compassionate observer, more in alignment with your authentic self than the part.

When you don't understand the purpose or function of a part, such as one that belittles you endlessly making you feel like complete garbage, ask this part, *what are you trying to do for me?* You can ask your parts anything that you want or need to know. Most parts want to be seen and heard and will share their story immediately. However, some hide and block other parts. A blocking part is like a wall; it stands in front of other parts or memories so that you can't see what is on the other side. This, of course, is another form of protection.

One important thing to know is that you don't have to get rid of parts. If they are ready to let go of what they're hanging onto then wonderful, then release with Love and appreciation. However, if a part isn't ready to let go, you can ask it to step back, soften, and get out of your driver's seat. We have parts that create addictions, such as to food, alcohol, drugs, gambling, sex, whatever it is to cope with distress. These parts often cling to the behavior, not wanting to change because they are afraid that you cannot handle life without it. Have patience with yourself and all your parts. Thank them for the job they are trying to do for you, and when you need to, politely ask them to take a rest.

The more you are in alignment with your spiritual self, the more willing parts are to release their burden and patterns. They need to know your authentic self and trust that they can manage without the part doing its job. We will discuss ways to connect with your spirit soon, but for now keep this in the back of your mind. Spending time in alignment with your spirit will help all your parts heal and your soul to transform.

Ego the Victim

People stuck in a victim's mindset feel like life is always against them, they don't have power to change their circumstances. They feel that they're unlucky and doomed to a miserable existence. I've been there before—I know what a dark place that can be. And unfortunately, because you are magnetic, if this is what you believe, this is the experience you will create in your life. I am NOT victim blaming. I am talking about how I see the reality of our existence. We create our life with our vibration. To change your reality, you must change your vibration, and the best way I've found is to work with your parts.

Ego feels all alone, like it must do all the heavy lifting, so it is understandable why it can make you feel like life is out of you control. However, you are learning differently. You are awakening to your true potential. To transcend the victim's level of consciousness it is important to take a hard look at the sum of your parts, examine their function, where they come from, reasons they get triggered, and ways that you can work together for your highest good.

When you talk to your inner critic, or your fear, be gentle and curious. The best way to get a part to shut up or act out even more is to berate them. They are not trying to make our lives rotten—they are just trying to make us feel better, using something that worked in the past.

For me, eating ice cream to cope emotionally is a throwback to being a teenager with my friends and whenever we had boy troubles we went out and got ice cream to make ourselves feel better. It's also something you see in the movies and on television—women eating ice cream to soothe their troubled souls, it's probably where my friends and I got the idea. These behaviors from my past, along with my natural love of all things sweet, family patterns of over-eating, and past life energy created parts of me that cope with difficult emotions by eating food. I spent years living in shame because no matter how hard I tried, I couldn't stop myself from binge eating. I didn't know all the dynamics and energy patterns around my behaviors until I started doing internal exploration.

Getting to Know Your Parts Exercise

Ask a part you want to get to know to step forward and separate from the rest of you (i.e., the part of me that says I am worthless). Or just go inside and ask for any part that wants to be heard to present itself. Notice where you feel this part in or around your body. Direct your breath to this part of your body and gently encourage the part of you to separate.

- Does it have an image, color, shape, sensation, emotion, texture, temperature?

- How old is this part?
- How old does this part think you are?
- What is this part's role in your life?
- What is this part trying to do for you?
- How did this part come to be? What happened that created this part? Allow it to share the story with you.
- What is this part afraid of will happen if it does not do its job?
- Does this part want to do something else? Does it want to let go?

Just sit quietly asking questions and set the intention that you are open to the answers. If another part jumps in saying, "This is dumb, I feel so stupid asking myself questions," gently acknowledge that it's trying to help you not feel embarrassed and let it know you will be alright. Ask it to step back and watch quietly. Ask for only the part of you that you're trying to communicate with to step forward and separate.

Once you are done, thank the part for being with you, and make sure to send it a lot of Love.

Working with Parts

The more you do this exercise the easier it will be to separate parts, understand their goals, motivation, origins, and what they fear. Awareness is empowerment. When you can recognize when a part is being activated, you can acknowledge it and ask it to step back and soften. You don't have to continue to move through life unconsciously reacting to all of life's triggers.

It might be a good practice to keep track of your work with different parts in a notebook so that you can connect patterns and deeply explore the role that they play in your life. When you see how your parts react to triggers, you gain an understanding of your inner psyche and can make more intentional choices.

Visualization can be used to help manage ruminating thoughts. Most likely, there is a part involved in a looping and repetitive stream of consciousness. With something like this, you can ask the part to go to a room in your mind to take a rest. Create a space that is a peaceful environment to help them relax. I created the "Room of Requirements" in my mind, from the *Harry Potter* books. This room is a space that will meet whatever the part's need is at that moment. I've seen in my mind's eye a part reading a book and drinking a cup of tea before, while others paint, dance, or eat. Whatever that part of me needs, the special room in my mind provides it.

The Benefits of Opening Up

So far, we have been exploring ways of raising awareness, by getting to know your body, how energy moves through you, and connecting with your different parts of self. While you are expanding your consciousness, it is very important to remain in a curious state: open, quiet, still, and present. This allows your mind, body, and soul to give you the answers you are seeking.

If I am having an intense reaction to something and I am unsure why, I have learned that it is because a part is being activated. In these moments I have learned to breathe and bring my nervous system back into balance. After I am regulated, then I can open myself up for inquiry, and seek to understand the part of me that is being triggered. From there, I can ask about what is going on and what it needs. Creating this separation through openness helps us to hold multiple layers of consciousness at once. You can be with your parts and hear their story while gaining new insights to what hid in the dark. In these moments you take on a dual role—you are both the questioner, and the questioned.

To engage with your parts, first breathe, regulate, get curious, look within, and be compassionate. Your parts need to feel safe, supported, loved, and appreciated. Space for healing is created when you become aware of your unconscious mind, and accept all your parts, as is.

Journal Prompt

Pick a part and go through the *Getting to Know Your Parts* exercise

Brittany Rose

from earlier in the chapter. Journal about what you learned from the part and how you will use this information.

Another exercise you can try is to write a thank you letter to a part, giving it Love and appreciation for what it has done to protect you. You can also give this part permission to rest.

Authentic Self

The Truth of Who You Are

Your ego is just one aspect of your being. Your soul and authentic self are the two most evolved parts of you. Often, people use soul and spirit interchangeably—however, I see a difference between the two. Your soul is an eternal spiritual vessel that travels with you from lifetime to lifetime. This part of you experiences life and learns its lessons, carrying those lessons, karmic debts (energetic imbalances between souls), and challenges from one incarnation to another. If you did not learn a lesson, you will repeat it in another lifetime. However, you can work with your soul to heal and integrate the growth.

Your authentic self is what I will often also refer to as your spirit. This is the most highly aligned divine part of your being, connected directly to Source Energy (or God, Universe, Consciousness, All-That-Is, Creator—however you conceive the divine). Your spirit exists in a frequency of Love and while it can continue to grow and expand through your soul's experiences, it is perfect. It wants to help you align with its frequency for healing and guidance.

As mentioned previously, we exist in different dimensions. Your soul exists with you in the physical realm, and in the spiritual realm. You can open to your spirit's wisdom and guidance through the channel of your soul.

Your spiritual self has the benefit of seeing your life from an elevated perspective. Your personality parts can see only what is right in front of you and behind you. However, this higher level of consciousness can see opportunities, experiences, growth, perspectives, and resources that can be called into your experience from a much broader view. Your spirit is wise, loving, and compassionate. It will always guide you with kindness. It may not tell your parts what they want to hear but it will never be angry or hurtful. This is because your spirit is pure and eternal Love.

My Authentic Self

I often tell people the story of the first time I became consciously aware of my connection with my spiritual self. I was contemplating taking a job I REALLY wanted, but the circumstances were less than ideal. I was so anxious—it didn't feel right. I'd be part-time and have no guaranteed hours or benefits, with more driving. I planned on stocking up on non-perishables like excessive toilet paper and paper towels, in anticipation of my reduced income.

One day, while I was walking around the house cleaning, I experienced an urge to pick up a journal and start writing. When I did, I felt something come over me. A chill went through my body, and it was as if I had entered a trance, and someone else took over. I wrote in my journal:

Don't take the job, wait. The ideal circumstances will come to you if you are patient.

I was in complete awe. I knew deep in my bones that this was true and that I had to refuse the job, I couldn't take it the way it was being offered to me. This information was coming from something in me, that was deeper and truer than my twenty-seven-year-old self. However, parts of me felt frustrated because patience is not one of my strengths.

After receiving the guidance, I declined the offer and continued working in a job I didn't like. Exactly a month after I channeled this message to wait, I was called and offered the position full-time, with benefits, less driving, and a decent salary. Elated, I was so thankful I listened to my inner wisdom. It would take me a few more years before I really got to know her, but that was my first conscious connection with my authentic self.

My spiritual relationship developed more fully after I went to a holistic fair and found on the free used book table, a book that vibrated in my hands when I picked it up. I knew it was meant for me. *Spiritual Growth: Being Your Highest Self* by Sanaya Roman changed my life.[7] It is the third part in a series on spirituality. Sanaya wrote the book by channeling a spiritual being named Orin. By reading this book, I was able to make a conscious connection with my spirit, whose name, I'd later learn, is ChristiBella. The teachings and exercises helped me strengthen my connection with my spiritual self and be able to discern her guidance.

Connecting with Your Authentic Self

The method I use to connecting with my authentic self is very similar to connecting with parts. It is all about setting an intention. To begin, first turn your focus inwards. Ask your parts to step back and soften. Imagine a beautiful beam of light pouring in through the top of your head, and know that this is the light of your spirit. Feel yourself merging into your whole being and allow yourself to be open to your authentic self's love and wisdom. Sit in stillness and be receptive to your spirit's energy for as long as you feel called to.

There are many ways of connecting in—this works best for me. Try it out and if it doesn't resonate, set an intention to open to your authentic self, and trust you'll be guided to the best method for you.

Although I did not know it at the time, what I did when I channeled that message about waiting and not taking the job is called automatic writing. It is a common way for people to download spiritual guidance. This is now one of my favorite practices because it is the most effective way for me to tune in and bypass my thinking mind. Our minds can impede messages coming through clearly. Ego often fills us with doubt, and can block, change, or confuse messages.

When I want to practice automatic writing, I typically write in my journal a question about something I need guidance around. The questions might be:

-Is this thing aligned with my highest good?

-What do I most need to know today?
-What do I most need to know about a specific thing?
-How do I align/accomplish a specific goal?
-What is best for me to focus on right now?

After determining what I want to ask, I go inwards, take some breaths, then settle my mind and body. I will ask for my parts of self to take a step back and soften so that I can receive guidance from my authentic self.

Work on creating a consistent practice: every day, allow yourself a few minutes to open yourself to your spirit's guidance. There is not much you need to do other than set the intention, get quiet, and allow yourself to be open and receive.

Meditation

Opening to spiritual energy can sometimes be challenging. People who are more anxious, have experienced a lot of traumas and stress in their life often have difficulty slowing down and feeling comfortable with stillness. Be patient and gentle with yourself and allow yourself to make small incremental steps at your own pace.

Meditation is one of the best ways to practice allowing your mind to quiet and settle, so that you can tune into the frequency of the divine. If this is challenging, start small, or begin with something you feel more comfortable with. Guided meditations are a great way to get used to going within. Your mind has a focal point because you are listening to someone else's direction or story. I also encourage people, when they feel ready, to just be with their breath. Following your breath as it moves in and out of your body is an excellent mindfulness practice. In my opinion, it is the best technique to help you get used to going inside and opening your channel to the divine.

With this practice it is also important to know that your mind will wander. The most important part of a meditation *practice* is to notice your wandering mind and gently bring it back to where you have set your focal point—in this case, your breath. Part of the practice is also becoming accustomed to the discomfort that may arise when you do this. Consistency will help increase your tolerance for it. Your different parts might use this as an opportunity to unleash all the thoughts they have been holding back. The goal is to not resist and force these thoughts to go away. When you notice this happening, allow them to float away naturally, and then return your attention to your breathing.

Meditation and mindfulness played a role in being able to learn how to tune into my emotions, to gain awareness, and then figure out the best way to manage them. Meditation has helped me to be less reactive, slow down, pause, and then respond to whatever the situation may be. I also believe that I can connect with my spiritual self much more easily and quickly because of consistent meditation. As they say, *quiet the mind so your soul can speak.*

Ways to Open to Intuition

Intuition is the ability to understand the messages from Spirit and put the pieces of the puzzle together based on your awareness of yourself, energy, the environment, signs, symbols and synchronicities. Spirit sends you messages all day every day, but you need to be vibrating at an aligned frequency in order to understand them. Therefore, one of the most important things a person can do to better hear their intuitive guidance is to manage their energy. Raise your vibes, open your channel, and tune into spiritual wisdom.

If you are trying to open yourself up as a channel and you are in a dark place, it's difficult to connect with divine guidance. This is because you're not resonating at the same vibration as that guide. You are much more likely to hear your parts and mistake this for your spirit. The reason being is that when you feel down, your vibration is more aligned with fear. When you are in a calm or joyous state, then you're radiating the frequency of Love.

You don't have to guess where the guidance or message is coming from, you can ask. Ask internally, who is saying this to me, is this my ego or my spirit? I have a visual sign ChristiBella gave me that tells me whether it's my ego (frog image) or spirit (owl image). When I ask, I often see the answer in my mind's eye as one of the two symbols my spiritual self gave me. Go inside and connect with your higher self and ask for your two signs. Trust and be open to what comes through.

. . .

Aligning Your Vibration

Your vibration has a direct impact on your ability to connect with Spirit. Think of yourself as a wireless radio. The more that you expand your energy, the more equipped you are to tune into the same frequency to hear the messages from the spiritual realm.

Some people have difficulty with the concept of higher and lower vibration, worrying that this means lower vibration is bad. It is not bad, as all energies have a place and purpose. Although there is space for all emotions and energy, we are functioning at our most optimal levels when we resonate with Love, the highest vibration on the planet.

Some people find it better to think of vibrations as fast and slow rather than high and low. The things that will slow down your vibration include: negative thoughts, judgment, fear, anger, sadness, toxic foods/substances, and injuries. The things that don't really feel all that good.

There are many ways to raise your vibration. You need to experiment with what feels best for you. Engaging in natural, spiritual, meditative, joyous, loving, creative activities, and gratitude practices, are some examples of practices that will help you elevate your vibration and become more aligned with Spirit's frequency.

Feel into the energy around an activity or thought pattern. Does it feel spacious, joyous, open, or peaceful? Or does it feel heavy, dark and dense? If it's the former, that's a sign to go ahead! Or if it's the latter, you'll want to think about it.

It is important to recognize the differences between self-care practices and self indulgence. Self-care nurtures, cares for, and heals our physical, emotional, and spiritual wellness. Self indulgence is when we engage in behaviors that may feel good in some ways, but have a cost attached to them. Drinking alcohol can be fun, but getting wasted frequently and using booze to numb is self-indulgence and can be harmful. Sometimes it's not about what you do but how you do it.

Love is the most powerful, highest, or fastest frequency in the Universe, so doing what you Love, expressing Love, and thinking in loving ways all will help you match this energetic vibration. High vibration=clear channel for spiritual healing and guidance.

Tools

For many following a spiritual path, there exists an affinity for crystals. Crystal energy is a gift from Mother Earth. Their high vibrational frequencies can help transform our energy just by having them nearby. Trust your gut when it comes to crystals—choose ones you feel called to. Allow them to speak to you, to help you heal, expand, and grow.

Working with crystal energy is a beautiful and natural way of raising your vibration. Wear them as jewelry, carry them with you in your pockets, bag, or bra—I've been known to put them in there from time to time. You might create beautiful crystal grids to set intentions with, or program a crystal with a specific purpose. You can hold them during meditation or place them on parts of your body and ask to receive their healing frequencies. There are so many things you can do with crystal energy, and if you feel called to, explore this more!

When working with Spirit I love to have crystals either on me, in my hands, or nearby. Selenite is my favorite crystal. It is self-cleansing, and for me acts like a spiritual microphone, helping me channel messages more clearly. However, some may not resonate as well with selenite and may choose to work with amethyst, clear quartz or any other stone. Follow your inner guidance and allow it to help you select the ones most highly aligned with you.

Divination tools are often helpful as an intermediary between us and Spirit. If you feel called to work with tools such as tarot and oracle cards, runes, or a pendulum go ahead and experiment. Oracle cards are my go-to when I need more clarity or confirmation on the messages I am receiving. They can also be extremely helpful in illuminating subconscious blocks. We all have things that our ego parts try to prevent us from seeing, using oracle cards, runes, or a pendulum to ask questions can be useful to help enhance our intuition.

When working with any of these tools I first ask my parts of self to step back and soften, then I open and align with my authentic self. This is important because when you are exploring, you know what energy is responding to your inquiry and that it is aligned with your highest good. Once I feel connected, I ask my question. I don't follow any rules like "shuffling three times and then cutting the deck" or anything like that. I shuffle until I get a nudge to stop or sometimes a card falls out of the deck, and I know it's meant for me.

To read tarot or oracle cards, I always set the intention that my higher self will help me understand the meaning behind the cards I pick. Then I focus on the images and symbolism, the emotions it evokes in me, and the connections I see between situations in my life or the question I asked. Only after I sit in openness to receive the meaning for a while will I read the guidebook's interpretation of the card's energy. Sometimes I won't even look at it, it all depends on my gut feeling. I have found when working with oracle cards that sometimes reading the book just clouds my intuitive voice and makes my personality parts create different meanings. However, there are also times when the book will say something that really resonates and provides me with even more clarity about the answer to my question. Don't be strict with your rules for reading oracle cards, allow yourself to follow your knowing and see what happens!

A pendulum is a tool that has something like a crystal on the end of a chain or string. It rotates in a circular motion when you hold it straight up and down. The idea is that you can connect with your higher self or spirit guides and ask yes or no questions. The spiritual energy will move the pendulum in the direction (clockwise or counterclockwise) to answer whether it is a yes or a no. Sometimes people connect with the spirits of the departed through this tool.

Many people are successful using pendulums for divinations. I, unfortunately, have found out the hard way that my pendulums often tell me what I want to hear. I know other people who deeply connect with this tool and say that their pendulum has its own personality and consciousness.

Sometimes I use one to clarify what I truly want, and since it is responding to my energy, in this situation it works. However, those wanting to use it for divination, I believe that the best way to connect with this tool is to clear it and then set the intention that it aligns with your authentic self. To clear any item, you can smudge it with palo santo or sage smoke or you can hold your hands over it and express an intention that the object release any lower vibrational energy and align with the light and Love of your spirit.

I always ask the pendulum to first show me yes and show me no, as it can change from time to time. Once getting a sign of yes and no I then ask my questions. Pendulums can also be helpful in finding lost objects. In this situation, it's almost like playing a game of hot or cold. Yes means keep going in that direction, no means nope you're getting cold.

When working with intuitive guidance, don't stop at the first answer. Whether you're talking with your parts, spiritual self, guides, or working with divination tools, it is always okay to seek clarity. Just because you get the tower card in a tarot reading doesn't mean your life is over. It means something is dismantling, but there's also an opportunity for you to rebuild. The next question you can ask is, how do I move through this tower moment with ease? Or, how do I align with my soul's highest path?

Get in the practice of being curious like a child and always dig to the deeper layers of who, what, where, how, and why. If I want to understand myself, my life, my circumstances better, I have to investigate. Sometimes the answers are difficult and not always what you want to hear. That's okay, be kind and gentle with yourself. Having more information is always empowering.

Unblocking Your Intuition

In the beginning of learning how to connect inwards with your authentic self, some feel like the channel is blocked. There are several things that you can do to help yourself release and heal the blocks.

First, ask yourself—which part of me is blocking my intuition? What am I afraid of happening if I hear my spirit's guidance? See where you feel the block, see if any images come to mind and if you hear anything in your mind. If a part steps forward, listen to it, listen to the fears and worries. Try to validate it, ask your spirit to step in and give it support if needed.

Sometimes these parts just need to meet your authentic self to feel safe enough to unblock you. They are trying to protect you and perhaps they felt disconnected, or they don't even really know that this spiritual part of you exists. Once they know there is someone better equipped to handle the situations they feel responsible for, often parts will release their burden and let the authentic self take over.

Although it is best to involve parts when you can, there are other ways to unblock yourself. As you will continue to see throughout, the work I do is always through setting intentions to direct the flow of energy.

To expand your consciousness, go inside yourself, and connect with your authentic self. Set the intention to release all blocks to your connection. Ask that these blocks both known and unknown to you be released from your mind, body, souls, cells, DNA, vibration & every aspect of your being. Ask that they be transmuted back into pure Love and light.

I like to cover all my bases when I set an intention.

Meet Your Authentic Self

Connect with your spirit as often as possible. You can even combine this practice with automatic writing.

Get into a comfortable position. Begin focusing on your breath and close your eyes if that feels comfortable for you.

Notice your body relaxing as a feeling of peace and calm flows over you. Relaxing your head and face, moving down your neck and relaxing your shoulders.

You are breathing deeply and easily, and this sense of relaxation moves down your chest and arms. Relaxing the core of your body.

You continue to breathe deeply, as you notice your hips and legs are relaxing. The calmness moves down into your calves, and finally relaxes your feet.

You are completely at ease. Set the intention for your parts to rest, relax, and allow you to be open.

Now you imagine a beautiful beam of light shining down from the heavens. It surrounds you and flows into your head, spreading down and throughout your entire body.

You are connected to your most authentic self. Feel the energy of this union harmonize your mind, body, spirit. Healing your cells, DNA, vibration, and every aspect of your being.

You now open yourself up to a message from your spiritual self. Be open to the message however it comes through.

Allow yourself to come back when you are ready.

Conscious Connection

Your authentic self wants to Love, support, and guide you. However, you have to be intentional and invite your spirit's presence. Your ego is loud, your authentic self is quieter. If you're asking about something and you get an immediate loud response in your mind, check again, chances are that's a part talking to you. If you discover it is a part, ask it to step back, and invite your higher self in once more. Your higher self comes through more clearly when your ego is settled.

Spirit wants what is best for you and is always trying to guide you towards this most aligned path. However, they will only intervene if you ask for help. Get in the habit of spending time daily connecting with your spirit for wisdom. Next we'll explore how to use Love from Spirit to heal your parts, and co-create the life of your dreams.

Healing

Reiki is Love, Love is Wholeness, Wholeness is freedom from disease. - Mikao Usui

If our thought and energy patterns can create illness and disease in our bodies, then changing thought and energy patterns can heal these issues. That sounds very simple, and it is once you understand the foundations of energy healing.

The goal of spiritual healing is to transcend from a level of victim consciousness, fear-based ego way of living to an empowered, loving, soulful life. Healing is an intentional act, one that your mind, body and spirit must agree upon. You must also align your actions with healing efforts. You cannot just receive healing—you must embody it. Healing is not a passive act. It requires changing thoughts, feelings, behaviors, and embracing Love.

Your thoughts, feelings, and behaviors all translate into vibration and that vibration dictates your physical, emotional and spiritual wellness. Although it is understandable that you might not feel in control of your healing, I assure you that you are. That does not mean you abandon conventional treatments and therapies. It can be supportive to include spiritual and energetic modalities along with your traditional treatments. One need not exclude the other.

When you are struggling, it may be useful to connect with your system and find out what part of self is involved. What function does being unwell serve? What's this part's role? Is it easier in some ways, or perhaps just more familiar? Is there an underlying benefit that is difficult to acknowledge? Do you feel that people expect less from you when you're sick? Maybe this healing will push you out of your comfort zone, so staying stuck, although uncomfortable in its own ways, keeps you from feeling even more discomfort in other ways.

As you uncover the layers of self it is important not judge yourself and these parts of you. Taking a mindful stance is a step towards finding inner peace. Mindful observance is the ability to see things as they are without attaching labels to them that place them in categories of good or bad. Your part isn't really trying to be a jerk when it berates you for fumbling over your words at your work meeting. It thinks it's *helping* to make sure you don't embarrass yourself again. Strange, I know, but this part learned that trick from somewhere. It thinks this technique works, so it continues to do it to protect you. There isn't a good or bad part, they just each serve different purposes. It is important to learn more about them to help facilitate healing.

Do not judge yourself for how you are now, this will prevent healing from taking hold. Love the beautifully imperfect mess you are today. Breathe in acceptance of who you are, who you were and who you're going to be.

LOVE

Love is the answer to all questions. Well, that's a bold statement, Brittany. Why is that, and what does that even mean? I received this powerful message during my Reiki master level training. It is the deepest truth I know and has become my mantra for life. *Love is the answer to all questions* means that Love is the highest frequency of the Universe. Seeing through the eyes of Love and being in the energy of Love, always changes our circumstances for the better. To heal, and align with your highest good, you must tap into your internal well of Love. It's there, a part of everyone and everything. Allow yourself to open to it, feel it, experience it, and set intentions with this creative force. This is how you embody Spirit.

No matter the situation, no matter the circumstance, no matter the person you encounter, the answer is always to send and embrace Love. We radiate Love through kindness, compassion, curiosity, patience, joy, and gratitude.

Open to Love by simply stating an intention: *I open my heart and mind to the presence of Love.* Say whatever feels right to you, but setting the intention will allow Love to flow. It's not just an emotion, it's an energy, it's a vibration, it's a force of creation.

Love is our natural state of being. It is the energy from which we came, and the energy from which we will return. In this physical world we experience other vibrations such as fear, anger, sadness. Even though we experience these other frequencies, at the core of all energy and all matter is the same essence of Love.

We all have the ability and capacity to experience joy, passion, creativity, and compassion. However, fear creates resistance, which prevents us from being in alignment with divine Love. We create blockages from interacting with lower vibrational energy—traumas, negative thought patterns, distressing experiences, injury, chemicals, and unaligned behaviors. Blockages are the walls that keep the divine presence of Love out. I will teach you how to how to release the resistance and the blockages for your energy's natural flow.

Forgiveness

One pathway to Love is through the intentional practice of forgiveness. When you hold on to anger, hurt, resentment and frustration you create energetic disturbances in your system, which can lead to disease. Anger and resentment become poisonous when it is held onto for long periods of time. Often, you must forgive someone else for your own good, rather than the benefit of that person. When you can forgive, and release the pain that you've been carrying, then you can heal and return to harmony.

Forgiveness is not always easy. When it is especially difficult for me, there are a few things I try to think about. First, it is my belief that everyone is always doing the best that they can in every moment. However, our best is fluid and changes.

When someone hurts me, I look at this as a reflection of their struggles. Don Miguel Ruiz's book, *The Four Agreements*, changed my life when I learned about and accepted the second agreement; *don't take anything personally.*[8] Once I read this chapter, my perspective on the behavior of others changed. If someone snapped at me for asking a question, I stopped believing it was because I was an idiot, instead I thought maybe they were having a bad day. Instead of internalizing negative thoughts and beliefs about me, I try to send the other person love so that they may heal. This helps me heal too.

I have had to enact a lot of forgiveness over the past two years. I've had to forgive myself for acting out of alignment with my most authentic self. And I've had to forgive my ex-husband for how he treated me during our marriage. I had to decide that I was going to see the relationship and the harm involved from a different perspective. Through therapeutic and spiritual healing work, I could see the interplay between past life karma, current family patterns, and trauma. This created unhealthy dynamics that became ingrained over almost two decades of being a couple.

The work was to shift my perspective of blame and victimization, to understand at a deeper level why things happened the way they did. It helped me be able to release anger and resentment and move to forgiveness and compassion for both of us. It was difficult in the relationship to not take my ex-husband's behavior personally. But once I was away from it, I could see how his actions reflected him and his wounds and did not mean I was a terrible person.

We are all connected at a spiritual level. This divine connection between All-That-Is helps me to remember that we are Love and light at our essence, regardless of how energy in the physical realm manifests. We all come from the same source. We are all worthy of connection and compassion. Therefore, if someone is struggling, if someone is making choices I do not agree with, instead of holding them in judgment, I try my best to hold them in Love.

That does not mean there is no accountability for their actions. I just believe there is a way to hold people accountable and be compassionate while doing so. I'm not perfect and this is a practice— meaning, something you must come back to and continue to work on. The more you're healed and loving towards yourself, the easier it is to love and not

39

judge others. I have learned how to do this with my ex-husband. I wish him nothing but positive things and send Love for healing and alignment with his highest good often.

Awareness of triggers is important because it is a clue where we need to do some healing work. Our relationships and reactions to others reflect our inner world. We attract people into our life based on the vibration we send out. 'Your vibe attracts your tribe' isn't just a cute saying, it's true. If you want to have healthier relationships, heal yourself and align with healthy connections, and part of that healing is through forgiveness.

Holding on to anger does not punish the other person. Sometimes people believe that burning with rage towards the person who caused harm keeps them safe from being hurt again. However, there's a different way of protection. If you establish compassionate boundaries with others, meaning, you don't tolerate abuse but set these lines down with Love and respect, then you are not as vulnerable to being hurt.

It doesn't mean it won't ever happen. But really think about it: do you need an intense reminder of the pain someone else caused? Or do you think you can integrate the lesson without having to poison yourself in the process? I really cannot answer the question for you. Your answer might differ from mine. That is fine, that is just where you're at right now. I just hope someday you're able to feel safe enough to let go of the hurt from others. You don't deserve to carry that pain around with you for the rest of your life.

Sending Love to those you disagree with is one of the most difficult and yet beneficial things you can do. To Love someone is to see that person for who they truly are—the innate goodness of their spirit and recognize their challenging behaviors as coming from human hurts and pain.

In all difficult situations, express compassion and intend for divine energy to support their healing and to encourage their remembrance of Love. Sending Love does not translate to continuing a toxic or unhealthy relationship. It is wishing them well on their journey, and praying for their healing as you part ways in the physical realm. Anger, hatred and resentment has never encouraged a person to heal and grow.

Only Love, compassion and kindness can do that. In all situations, no matter the situation, radiate Love.

Forgiveness Exercise

Think about someone you are ready to forgive. Get into a relaxed state and set the intention to do forgiveness work towards the specific person. Ask to align with your spiritual self.

Ask for support from your spirit to see this situation through the eyes of Love. Intend that this will elevate your perspective. Allow yourself to be open to this shift.

State an intention of willingness to forgive the person. Imagine sending them forgiving energy.

Ask for your authentic self to help you release this hurt (pain, trauma, resentment, anger, hatred), towards the other person and this situation/experiences. Imagine it is being pulled out from your cells, your DNA, your mind, body, soul, vibration, and every aspect of your being.

Release the hold it has on you. Release the impact it has, letting go of anger and fear.

After this feels complete, imagine that you are filling yourself up with healing light. You are radiating with compassion for yourself and the other person.

Send this love back out to the person with kindness, warmth, and compassion, wishing them well on their own soulful journey. Let them know that all is well between you and that although you may stay separated in the physical world, energetic healing has occurred for the highest good of all.

Ask for this healing energy to integrate into your mind, body, soul, cells, DNA, vibration and every aspect of your being.

Once this feels complete, consider journaling about your experiences.

Self Forgiveness

Self forgiveness is both essential and particularly challenging. Part of healing is learning to love and accept yourself, along with being able to forgive yourself for your imperfections. Often, people must unlearn ingrained harmful beliefs and release feelings of guilt, shame, anger, and resentment towards themselves. If you believe that what I said is true about other people, that everyone is worthy of Love, connection and compassion, that applies to you too.

You can repeat the forgiveness exercise above for yourself. I'd also encourage you to write out a self forgiveness statement. This serves as an intention that you are setting, a pathway for energy to flow towards releasing and healing these wounds. Once you set the intention, then you must step aside and allow the forgiveness to take hold. Here is an example of a self-forgiveness statement that you might make. I recommend you write your own—one that resonates with your soul.

I forgive myself for all my actions and deeds that were unkind to myself and others. I am ready to release the anger, hurt, pain that I have inflicted upon myself. I embrace Love in my heart towards myself and all others.
I release, I release, I release, and I forgive.
Thank you, and so it is.

After writing your forgiveness statement, or saying it out loud, take a deep breath, and imagine connecting with your spiritual self. Ask that they share Love and light with you, helping the healing take hold.

Self Love

You must turn your Love inwards so that you can spread it outwards. If you are constantly pouring from an empty cup, you will become depleted. Therefore, filling yourself up with Love is crucial to being able to help be present and to support others. Plus, my beautiful divine souls, you deserve to Love yourselves just because. You are worthy of care, respect, and nurturance just like everyone else. To be in alignment with your most amazing authentic self, it is important to Love all your parts, imperfections and all.

If you also think about it from an energetic perspective, you can see that we are all connected—we are all one from the same divine source, just translated into different physical forms. However, if you raise your vibration through loving yourself more, you impact everyone else on a collective level. You are drawing more light energy into this Universe, thus helping everyone rise, evolve, and heal.

If caring for yourself is difficult, go inwards and explore this. Talk with the parts involved, the ones that yell at you and say self-Love and self-care is selfish. Get to know their fears and then decide what you want to do with them. You can hear them out and help them release their burdens, which helps you become a healthier, happier, and more spiritually aligned version of yourself.

Where do we learn we are unworthy of Love? For many, this begins during childhood. When this happens, it is easy to internalize the belief that we are not lovable or not worthy of loving ourselves. Or that our worth is conditional on something.

You can start loving yourself more by following your inner guidance, and engaging in practices that are healthy for you. Reinforce this self-Love by thinking, feeling, and behaving in ways that make you feel sparkly inside. When you are full of Love, you are vibrant, and you can't help but share this energy with others. This is not selfish, it is how you can make a difference in the world, by being your happiest and healthiest self!

Everyone questions their purpose. I think it is a lot less complicated than we are led to believe. I believe it is to experience and share Love. Everyone's form of Love will look different, but essentially following your purpose means you go towards what lights up your soul, what causes your heart to sing. When you feel that way, keep exploring it. That is one reason that I'm writing this book. Writing gets me into the creative flow, which is my favorite feeling. I feel like I am electric when I create.

If you feel it is selfish to take care of yourself, then I encourage you to reflect on why that is. For each person it might be different. Maybe you had an overly critical mother or fell into a care-taking role at a young age. There might be a million different reasons why it's difficult to give to yourself. What I am here to say is it is possible.

I struggled for most of my life with accepting myself—my appearance, my personality, my quirks, I thought they were all wrong. I

43

thought I didn't fit in, that I wasn't good enough, smart enough, pretty enough. In an attempt to make myself feel more worthy, I gave, and I gave, and I gave to others to the point of depletion, and I was miserable.

Then I decided: I didn't want to live like that anymore. I started doing my work by going to therapy, learning reiki, spending hours meditating, reading a million (not really, but close) personal development books. I started giving (a little) less to others, and more to what filled me up. I threw myself deep into exploring the topics that resonated with me. I bask in learning about the Akashic Records, exploring manifestation practices, energy, and all things spiritual. This is my path—it is what I've done because of my soul's guidance. I follow my feelings of excitement to lead me to the next thing. I have literally picked books up and had them vibrate in my hands as if to say, "Yes, me, pick me!" The more you learn to tune into your own inner knowing, the more you will know exactly where to go and what to do.

Don't feel discouraged if it is difficult for you to tune into yourself still. It can be hard for many people, especially people who have learned it is safer to be disconnected. There is a way to go forward. It may take time, so have patience, compassion, and understanding with yourself. Your pace is perfect for you. I am still on this journey. Each day that I show up and do my own emotional and spiritual work, the deeper my Love for myself grows. Love is infinite and our embodiment of it can always expand.

Self-Love cannot depend on anything less than our true, authentic, spiritual selves. Your worth cannot be measured upon how others perceive you. As sad as it is, no one else other than you can or will be a constant in your life. Even your most beloved people will come and go. You cannot depend on them to give you worth, acceptance, or Love. They can certainly add to the beauty in our lives, but it is not fair to ask anyone to give us what we are unwilling to give ourselves first. This is how people can become too dependent, which can unfortunately sometimes push people away.

This is not to say shut people out either, not at all. We need connections with others, it just cannot be the only thing that sustains us. We need to find that within first and then look for it outside of ourselves. If this is you, breathe and shower yourself with kindness. It will be alright.

You're raising your awareness— you're both learning and growing. Soon you'll be blooming.

It can be done. Find your path, follow your light. Learn how to tune in and open yourself up to the Love within. Be kind, be gentle, be supportive, be nurturing, be all the things you wish other people were for you. Start today, start now.

Self Love Guided Meditation

Take a deep breath in through your nose, and out through your mouth. As you inhale, invite in relaxation, as you exhale release any stress or tension you are holding in your body. With every inhalation feel a sense of calmness spreading throughout your entire being. You are at peace.

Bring your focus inwards, allowing your breath to come in and out of your body. Inhale... exhale. Inhale...exhale.

Imagine that your heart is opening wide and brimming with light. You are opening to your most authentic self. This is the part of you that is the source of Love in your being.

Through this connection with your higher self, Love pours into you. It meets every single part of your being with compassion and grace. Feel this beautiful energy wash over you, covering you with warmth, peace, and Love.

Your authentic self wants you to internalize these beliefs. Soak in the vibration of these words.

I am good enough.

I am a beautiful soul.

I am a wonderful person.

I am worthy of Love.

I am capable.

I am valuable.

I love who I am.

I love who I was.

I love who I'm becoming.

I love and accept every part of me.

I am at peace with myself.

6

Brittany Rose

> I am proud of myself.
> I am confident in myself.
> I am my most authentic self.
> I am open to Love.

Feel the energy of Love help align you with these words. Allow the transformation to take place. Set the intention that the healing integrates into your mind, body, soul, cells, DNA, vibration and every aspect of your being.

At a time that feels right and comfortable to you, allow yourself to come back to your body, and then back into the room. If you feel called to, journal about your experiences.

Release, Heal, Embrace & Integrate

The Release, Heal, Embrace & Integrate (RHEI) is a healing process using energy and intention. You do not need to have formal training in any kind of energetic healing modality to benefit from enacting RHEI. However, learning to work with energy more in depth, such as learning Reiki and/or working in the Akashic Records may amplify your healing practices.

Through a combination of classes and my spiritual self, ChristiBella, I learned how to use this modality. It is now the foundation of the work I do with myself and my clients. And to be honest, we've already used RHEI in some of the exercises, it's that integral to how I heal. There are four steps that flow together creating a beautiful transmutation ritual.

Release is the first step of the process. It means setting the intention to let go of the energetic pattern, the need for the problem, and the unaligned vibrational energy associated with a specific issue. By setting the intention you signal that you are ready for it to change, to let go, and make space and room for something new, and more highly aligned with your soul's highest path, purpose, and potential. I like to release energy into an energetic container, such as a fire, a ball of light, the center of the earth, or a pool of healing water. My authentic self always shows me which element to use for each healing. Once it is in the

46

container, I ask for the Universe to transmute it back to pure Love and light.

There are a lot of different ways to do the releasing and clearing process. You could imagine roots growing out of the bottoms of your feet, reaching down into the core of Mother Earth. Send the energy down into the center, to be aligned with the highest vibration of Love and Light. I also often visualize energy clearing through fire, most likely because I am trained in Holy Fire Reiki. But you could use any elements or even a beam of any colored light to release any energy that no longer serves you. Go with what feels right. You can also visualize energy clearing in a physical space using the same intentions and elements.

The second step in this process is to set the intention to receive healing energy from the Universe. With this, you harmonize your mind, body, and soul into a state of peaceful equilibrium. I visualize healing light flowing into me and wrapping around my entire physical and energetic body. I allow the energy to flow for as long as it feels right.

Embrace is the third step. This refers to taking in the frequencies you wish to align with. It can be Love, light, consciousness, health, wealth, abundance, freedom, joy, or creativity. If you can imagine it, you can align your energy with it. Just ask your authentic self what vibrations are best for you to align with and you will be guided.

Integrate is the last step. I do this by setting the intention that Spirit integrates the energy shifts into my mind, body, soul, cells, DNA, vibration, and every aspect of my being with ease. Then I sit and just simply allow it to happen. With this last step, sit in the stillness of your soul for as long as you feel called to, allowing your energy field to recalibrate, harmonize, open, and align with the vibrations of your highest good.

When you work with this process, it is crucial to allow Spirit to guide you. Feel into if you are trying to control anything. If something comes up, set the intention to release the need for control. Truly, let God take the wheel. In this book, I give you several meditations to get you used to the process. However, if while you're in meditation and you experience something completely different from what I guided, just go with it. Trust the divine wisdom of your authentic self over any personality, any writing, any other person's teachings. Your needs for healing are different from mine. Some people will resonate with my methods, others will not. All of this is just as it should be. There is no judgment. We are just vibrating at different frequencies, neither right nor wrong, only right or wrong for you.

You can use RHEI for any kind of healing. Do you want to heal a physical ailment? Release the energy around this physical ailment. Do you have anxiety about something? Release, heal and embrace new beliefs about the situation. A problematic relationship? RHEI it. This is of course in conjunction with any medical or mental health treatment that is right and appropriate for you. Energy healing is in addition to, not in lieu of, more traditional forms of treatment.

Louise Hay taught in her book, *You Can Heal Your Life,* how if you have any kind of issue, simply saying, "I release the need" for it will allow the energetic patterns associated with the problem to let go. For example, if you have an earache you would say, "I release the need for this ear pain and any other associated ailments." I always allow my intuition to guide me to the right words and often repeat it or at the very least say "I release, I release, I release." And then I follow it up by drawing in healing energy and embracing a healthy, harmonious ear and hearing.

Louise Hay's book talks about how there are emotional causes to each of our physical ailments. Therefore, the way to embrace a new energy is to get to the root of the emotional problem. I genuinely turn to this book if I have any kind of physical issue, to understand why it is happening, and the words I can speak into my existence to help it align with a different vibration.

When working with your parts to heal using RHEI, it is essential that you let the part direct the healing. Some parts are not ready to let go of their burdens, even if you want them to. Meet this part with Love and compassion, and let them know they can release when they're ready to.

Sometimes, it takes more than one round of RHEI to fully transform an issue. You'll see this portrayed later on in my journal entries. I worked with a part to release a burden and then the same part, just a different aspect of it, popped up again a few days later. This is normal, healing happens in small steps, not huge leaps. Be patient with yourself, and know that the more you connect with your authentic self, the safer your parts are going feel to let go.

· · ·

RHEI Meditation

For this meditation you are going to want to get yourself comfortable, relax your body, settle your mind, and ask for your parts to step back and soften so that you can be open to your authentic self.

Take some nice deep breaths in and out, focusing on your breathing. Relaxing more with each inhalation and releasing stress and tension with each exhale. Continue to breathe in and breathe out until you feel completely relaxed.

Now, I want you to bring to mind a specific problem or belief you would like to alter. Ask your system to help you understand the problem or belief.

Once you are more aware, invite your parts to release this problem or belief from your mind, body, soul, cells, DNA, vibration every aspect of your being.

Imagine the problem is going into one of the elements. You could release it to water, air, the earth, a giant fire, or a beam of spiritual light. See yourself letting go of the issue from your energy system and intend that it is transmuted back into pure Love and light.

Set an intention to receive healing Love and light from the Universe. Feel this energy flowing into you, bringing you back to harmony.

It is time to embrace fresh energy and new beliefs. Call in those intentions now. Ask for your spiritual self to guide you to align with the energy that serves your highest good.

Ask that this energy is integrated into your mind, body, soul, cells, DNA, vibration, and every aspect of your being.

Take your time and at a pace that feels comfortable for you, come back into the room. If you feel called to, journal about your experiences.

Clearing Techniques

Similar to releasing energy, there are many ways to clear your energy. Clearing or releasing does not mean the energy disappears, because energy cannot be created, nor destroyed. Clearing in this context means that its vibration shifts and there is a restoration of the natural flow of energy. As we go about our lives in the world, we accumulate energy from those around us, the environments we are in, and the emotions we experience. Clearing unaligned energy is essential for wellness.

My favorite way to transmute energy is through what we just discussed in RHEI, using an intention and visualization. I might say, I *release any excess energy unaligned with my highest good, and transmute it back into pure Love and light*. This is an intention you can easily use at any time and in any place.

Whenever I am thinking negatively, I try to catch myself. I sometimes will say "Stop. Clear, Clear, Clear". This intention cleanses the energy of the words I just spoke upon my life. I then counter it with a different affirmation of the energy and intentions I wish to draw into my experience.

More traditional clearing practices involve people smudging their energy field and space with smoke from sage or palo santo. The smoke has cleansing properties that transmute energy to a neutral vibration. Scientific research has been done on this. The Journal of Ethnopharmacology published a research study proving that the smoke clears the air of bacteria, thus changing its natural vibration.[9]

Some crystals are cleansing and elevating. Selenite is a highly cleansing crystal. I'll use a selenite wand much like one would use sage smoke, running the wand through my energy field. Because I am so in tune with my system, I can immediately notice a difference in my vibration.

Energy Filter

Another practice that can be helpful for sensitive people is to create energetic boundaries. Many spiritual teachers will instruct people to block the energy of others by setting an intention to place a protective energetic barrier around you. This may be helpful for some— however, it was never helpful for me. The natural state of energy is to flow, and creating a barrier to that flow does not feel aligned with my inner guidance. My Reiki teacher, Mary Riposo from Infinite Light Center, taught me a visualization: to feel myself as if I was clothes hanging on a clothesline, and to allow the emotional energy of others to blow through me as if they were being moved by the wind. This did not stop the energy from entering but allows it to pass through me and not remain stuck in my body.

My Akashic Records teacher, Emily Jean Blatt from Awaken and Ground, showed me how to create an energetic filter rather than a barrier around me. I set an intention that the energy I receive passes through a filter of love, light, and consciousness and is sent back the same way. This diffuses the emotional intensity of the energy I feel, but I am still aware of it on some level. For me, I need this, as I am a therapist and being able to feel and empathize with my clients' experiences is important. However, becoming overwhelmed with their emotions is not helpful. Therefore, this filter helps me to protect my heart while still allowing me to remain open to the natural flow of energy between myself and others. I do this by intention and setting and visualizing an energy filter activating all around me.

The intention I set for this is:

Spirit, please create an energetic filter of love, light, and consciousness all around me so that all energy I receive from others passes through this filter, and the energy I send back out also passes through the filter of love, light, and consciousness. Thank you, thank you, thank you.

It's wordy, I know, but it's what came to me naturally. If those words don't work for you, take this concept and create your own intentions that work for your soul.

Journal Prompts

Go through the forgiveness exercise. How do you feel towards the person now? What shifted?

Do the RHEI exercise. What came up to be healed? What happened during your healing? Do you notice a shift around the situation?

Alignment

Match the Frequency You Want to Live

On this journey, so far, you have learned how to illuminate the blockages in your soil that prevent growth. You now know how to release these blockages and nurture your soul so that you can plant new seeds of desires. That's what this chapter is about. Planting seeds that bloom as you transform.

Spiritually Guided Creation

By developing a relationship with your spiritual self, you have the benefit of asking to see the highest vision for a certain aspect or part of your life. It is helpful to ask for guidance with your creations. When you quiet your mind and enhance your intuition, you are better able to follow the spiritually directed path.

Ask Spirit to give you information about the highest potential for your life. What are some ways for you to reach this highest ideal? What are the best action steps for you to take to align with your highest good and the highest good of all? It would be helpful to connect with your authentic self and automatic write the answers to these questions.

. . .

Matching Frequencies

You already know the power of intention—you have seen how it's helped with releasing and healing. If you want to manifest something, you need to speak it into existence in your life. Talk about it, write about it, think about it, feel it. You must live in the energy you want to manifest. If you want to open a bakery and become your town's favorite baker, then you need to bake a lot, surround yourself with baking resources and tools, associate with other people who like to bake, and watch videos and listen to podcasts about baking. But the most important part of all of this is you must believe in yourself and your ability to be successful.

Alignment is about getting your energetic frequency to match your desired outcome. Like calls to like. If you want a happy, healthy, prosperous life, your energy must resonate with these elements to draw them into your experience. You must create situations that reinforce happiness, health, and abundance. It might be going to a concert you friends, exercising and eating healthy, or circulating resources with Love.

While it is easy to brainstorm ideas on how to be in the energy you wish to manifest, sometimes there are other factors that need to be addressed. There are experiences, beliefs, and other influences that often prevent you from manifesting. Recognizing the blocks to bringing certain things into your life like love, abundance, or health, will allow you to enact healing and then align your energy with the new reality. Use your awareness tools to discover the blocks, and then go through the steps of RHEI to transmute unaligned energy.

Affirmations

Alignment takes intentional thoughts and actions. There is no one right way to align with what you want, but there are many practices that can be helpful. Affirmations are a simple and effective way of aligning your energy with a new belief. They are statements about the shifts you want to create. *I am,* are two of the most important words a person can say. These two words are a way to communicate with your spiritual self the energy you wish to embody.

I am good enough. I am smart. I am capable. I am prosperous. I am healthy. I am loved and loving. I am living my best life. Notice how your body feels when you say these positive affirmations. If you notice resistance or tension as you speak these words, then you've found yourself a blockage. Investigate by going inside and understanding the belief, and then work with your system to release, heal, and embrace aligned energy.

Align Your Actions

It is essential when consciously manifesting to not only align your vibration but to align your actions. You can do all the rituals and manifestation techniques in the world, but if you do not put in the actual labor to change, then it will not matter. You will just be wishing and wanting rather than aligning and having.

I dreamed of being a writer for a very long time. The process of getting to where I am right now, which is on track to finish this book, required me to gain awareness of the blocks from the many parts of my life—release and heal those parts, and align my frequency with courage, creativity, openness to Spirit's guidance, commitment, confidence, and passion. These characteristics have helped me keep going, to feel like I am no longer the one in charge but answering the Universe's call to birth this book into the physical realm. Writing does not feel like I have to force or push anymore. It flows.

However, I must show up at my keyboard each day and write. All the healing work in the world would be completely pointless if I did not start taking steps towards what I want to manifest. No one is going to drop a best-selling book in my lap and say, 'here you go, this is yours now.' Nope, I have to both align my energy AND consistently do the work.

Visualization

Jon Gabriel created a weight loss and health program focusing strongly on relaxation and visualization practices. I found The Gabriel Method when I weighed 300 pounds in 2021. I listened to the morning and evening meditations everyday for months. These meditations helped program my brain and body to want to lose weight, so taking action was easier. For the first time in my adult life, my entire system agreed that eating healthy and exercising was what was best for me. Because of a visualization program and reprogramming my energetic and emotional system, I was able to take the steps necessary to lose over 100 pounds.

Visualization uses the imagination, and the power of your imagination is vast. If you can imagine it, you can direct the flow of your energy to it. Imagination is just another form of intention. When you are imagining your manifestations coming to life, you also need to allow yourself to see what it would be like in your mind's eye and feel into the experience. Imagine what emotions you'd be experiencing. Joy, love, gratitude, peace, comfort, optimism. See it, think it, feel it, create it. Your brain cannot tell the difference between real and imaginary, and neither can the Universe. What you think, you create.

Imagine what you would do if you were living your dream life. What and who would be around you? What would your day look like? How would you feel? What would you think about yourself and your circumstances? Visualize your dream life, and hold the energy of the vision with you as long as possible. This is a beneficial strategy that can help you co-create a beautiful life.

Creative Manifestation

Creative energy is a powerful vibration that likes to be used to help manifest ideas into existence. There are so many ways of utilizing the physical environment to communicate to the Universe what you are trying to attract. People create vision boards, crystal grids, spells, and altars all in service of aligning with an energy to manifest a reality.

I love vision boards. I create multiple throughout the course of a given year. Plain notebook covers or planners are also great places to create a vision board. In my personal planner I add stickers, words of affirmation, and other symbols to help set the tone for what I want to resonate with. When I see these words and symbols, I give myself a moment to align my energy with their vibrations.

I also have a manifestation journal. In this journal I glue in images and words from magazines, or stickers representing the themes of what I am trying to manifest into my life. In the blank spaces in between images, I write affirmations and what I wish to create. The words are a way of scripting out my life, writing every sentence with gratitude in the present moment. It is important to affirm that this reality is happening for you right now. Matching the vibration of your vision allows the Universe to deliver the ideal circumstances and people to help you create the life you're asking for.

Crystal grids are another manifestation technique of mine that I love to use. Crystal grids use sacred geometric patterns such as the Flower of Life or Metatron's Cube as the base, and then you create a pattern with crystals on top of them, programming the crystals and grid with your intention. I often sit in front of my crystal grids, sending them Love while visualizing my intentions. You can manifest anything with this technique. Currently, I have a healing grid and altar up in my sacred space for my friend who is ill. I visualize Love and light giving her strength, removing blocks and barriers to the flow of her life force energy, and providing her with exactly what she needs for her highest good. When I created this grid, I put all my materials into different piles and allowed Spirit to guide me to the right crystals, the right grid, the right intentions to set in order to help support my friend's healing.

These practices are very enjoyable to me. Experiencing the flow of creative energy is, to me, better than any drug. The positive emotions I experience while creating enhances the vibration I am communicating to the Universe. It is always best to manifest while you are in a state of Love. Do this by thinking about things that make you feel joy and gratitude.

Let Spirit guide you when you are manifesting, to ensure you are not creating from a place of fear. Let your spiritual self inform the intentions you set and how you go about manifesting them, when you do this, you know you are manifesting from a place of Love.

If you are of a witchy persuasion or just love to do rituals, go for it! I love working with lunar energy and so will often do rituals around the times of the new moon and full moon. Let Spirit move you towards the manifestation practices that feel most aligned for your soul.

. . .

Journal Prompt

Write out your dream life. Write it as if it is happening in the present moment, giving details of who, what, where. Feel into this life and visualize it playing out in your mind. Express Gratitude to the Universe for this wonderful reality you are co-creating.

My Lunar Cycle of Growth
Soul Healing

This next section is a month of my healing journey, from new moon to new moon. I explore why I veered from my path. Using the practices and techniques I described in section one, I document how I open to my authentic self again. I begin the month emotionally distressed because of my job as a hospice social worker. The position consumed my life, and even when I was out of work I felt dragged down by the stress of an unhealthy system.

I wanted to chronicle this journey to show you what working with these techniques looks like. The next section is a grouping of journal pages I wrote to document my efforts, progress, and struggles. This is not a linear path because healing does not happen in a straight line. I write as I do the work, which can be messy and even chaotic. However, raw as it may be, it is very much authentic.

It's okay if healing is shambolic and does not follow a logical trajectory. Each time you work through something you create space for your beautiful, most authentic light to shine through. By the end of my month-long journey of purposeful healing, I am more open and aligned with my spiritual self. And I hope this book helps you to get there too.

June 16, 2023

New Moon

A new moon means new energy. I am so fucking ready. It's time to release all this pent-up anxiety, chaos, stress, anger, frustration, and fear. I've lived this life before, and there's no way I am going to stay in this vibration. Something needs to change.

As I connect with the new moon energy, I embrace peace, calm, Love, joy, creativity, health, abundance... with a side of freedom, please.

Tonight, I call out to the *New Moon*, the beginning of a new lunar cycle, and claim that I am manifesting a life that is aligned with my soul's deepest desires. A life that lights me up instead of pulls me down. One where I can shine my light and help others to shine theirs too.

I've repeated the cycle, hopefully for the last time. And what did I learn? I need to be my own boss and allowed to use my time and energy in ways that feel right for me. Chaos systems disrupt the peaceful energy I worked so hard to cultivate. I can only control my reactions to things so much before the energy of others throws me off course.

Being a helper is a huge part of my identity. But I want to help in ways that don't cause harm to me. I've been here before, a phase repeated, now revisiting this space for further growth. I can see it— therefore, I can heal it.

The time is now to seize my life again! To change what is unaligned with my highest good. To shift my mindset, and consciously create a different way of being.

Sometimes, according to Queen Kloee Taylor (my favorite YouTube tarot reader), we just need to smack ourselves on the ass and not think like that anymore! I need to stop being so negative, even though I am so frustrated where I am at. I am just feeding into the monster and falling deeper into darkness. Enough. I'm done. I'm shifting.

When the negative thoughts comes up, I need to stop and remember that I can release, heal, embrace and integrate.

Tonight. I need to work on weight release. It is so disturbing to me that I can work and work and work, and stress will prevent me from losing weight. But I know how to work with my energy through intention.

I ask for healing love and light to flow into me.
I ask to release all excess weight and all limiting beliefs about losing weight
from my mind, body, soul, cells, DNA, vibration,
and every aspect of my being.
I ask for this energy to be transmuted back into pure love and light.

I now embrace the energy of releasing excess weight with ease. I am at a
healthy weight for my body. My body is in perfect health.
I integrate this healing into my mind, body, soul, cells, DNA, vibration,
and every aspect of my being. Thank you.

I need to remember that just taking a few minutes to set intention and transmute energy can create powerful shifts in my being. These are the practices that are going to help me align more with my authentic self.

Feeling energy flow through my being is one of my greatest joys. I've missed it these last few months of disconnection. My soul craves and needs to be connected to the divine much more than I have been. Intentional practice and devoted time are necessary to heal and transform into my authentic self.

It is frustrating to go backwards, but the past has many valuable lessons. I'm moving forward now, with experience. This is my opportunity to deepen my growth.

Some of my most transformative healing has happened in water. I am the wateriest of water signs, and it is an excellent amplifier of energy. While taking a bath tonight, I asked to release all the energy I had absorbed from others. I immediately felt a pulling on my energy field. It was as if energy was being lifted from out of my body. It was so powerful it made me feel nauseous. I did it for as long as I could stand before asking Spirit to heal me and allow me to embrace Love, light, and consciousness.

The strength of the energetic exchange was intense. A sign to me that this a needed practice and I should do it much more frequently than I have. Step one: I need to work on release. It's time to clear the pathways for new, higher vibrational and more aligned energy to come through!

June 17, 2023

Awareness

I am inside my body, feeling the bubbling, gurgling, buzzing sensations activated throughout my system. The movement of energy makes its presence known throughout my being.

I call in the energy of Love to heal and harmonize me.
I ask for alignment with my spiritual self.

I have spent the day noticing what's happening inside of me and being present with my body's many dimensions of sensuality.

After work, I mindfully lifted weights. With every rep, I was aware of my muscles contracting and releasing. Followed up with a slow and steady yoga routine, stretching and strengthening my muscles. I carefully directed my attention to noticing the flex and flow of each movement.

Dinner was a fiesta in my mouth of Peruvian cuisine. Seafood drenched in bold flavors at interesting temperatures, and unfamiliar textures. It was an exploration of a culture that I am not familiar with, and I am intrigued by their representation through food.

We ended the evening with my favorite, Bubblecake. There's a delicious cookie sandwich I love. It is 'a once in a while' indulgence that brings me great joy. So today, I chose it. Tomorrow, and for many tomorrows after that I will not indulge. I enjoyed it immensely, and I will not feel guilty.

I can feel my system vibrate as I write these words. A nudge from Spirit that, in writing this, there is alignment for me. Enhancing awareness is something I need to continue to work on. Being present in my mind, body, and soul will assist me with embodying my wholeness.

June 18, 2023

Calling in Love

There's a heaviness to today, but even with its dense presence, I called in joy. I reveled in childlike wonder in the woods. I had fantastical moments of play along the Dinosaur Trail. Then we had hours of visual entertainment with the antics of the Flash.

The heaviness I felt was my partner silently suffering. Once I knew the problem, I helped him hold it, and shared my Love with him.

Far too often, he sees me sad and stressed because of work. His sadness lays more beneath the surface and I don't see it in him as much. I wanted to fix it but know the only thing I can really do is to be present, give him my Love, and hold space. I can understand the sadness he feels on Father's Day, with the complicated relationship he had with his.

Spirit, please send my soulmate healing Love and light.
Fill us both with your radiant energy.

Today is the actual new moon, and as I plant my seeds for manifestation, I am really trying to let Spirit take the wheel and guide my healing. I released energy absorbed by others again. It was less intense than yesterday, but still powerful.

Spirit guided me to talk to a part of me that likes to binge eat. Her

64

name is Big Bertha, and she eats for comfort—no surprise there. After a little convincing, and a lot of Love, she agreed to release the vibration around this behavior and her need to protect me in this unhealthy way.

I covered myself in crystals to help amplify the healing energy channeled. I asked to embody the energy of *Love, light, joy, peace, abundance, health, creativity, clarity, empathy, and compassion.*

I let the energy flow into me until it felt complete. Immediately afterwards I notice my brain is less foggy and my body is less sore.

The anxiety about work is still there, unfortunately. I am ready to be done with the pressure. I know I need to be done. And I will be... soon.

Spirit again guided me to another area of healing tonight. I worked with a part to release fear of work and financial insecurity. I know I am going to have to heal my relationship with money to make my dreams manifest into reality.

Before I jump off the cliff, I need to release these fears and trust that Spirit will not let me fall too far down. A net will appear, and I will know which way to go. It's how it has always been— it's how it will always be. Today I open my heart and embrace faith that the Universe has my back.

June 19, 2023

Choosing Me.

I've been through a lot in my lifetime, but the last two years have been especially tumultuous.

Last year when I was in the DDPY Positively Unstoppable Challenge, I begged God to give me a break. Let me win so I could use the money to take time off, breathe, regroup. Well, I didn't win, so as I planned to start my new life, I got a job. One completely new, but that I felt guided towards.

Now I realize, I had the opportunity the entire time, I just had to know where to look for the resources.

I am not my best self in this job. Hospice is sacred work, and although I think I do it with great Love, I feel my energy would be better elsewhere.

Even though I was trying to make it longer at this company, today I just knew. It's time to put in my notice and leave. Let myself be free. I choose me.

I was put in this position to see what I would do. Well, I stressed, and I got anxious, but I kept working on my health (mostly with DDPY and eating healthy). In this liminal state, I became depressed, disconnected from Spirit, and stuck in an uncompleted stress cycle.

A job will not destroy me. From the very beginning I knew that my long-term path was not with hospice. I am meant to work for myself, and to share Love, light, and consciousness with others.

In a lifetime of giving, I have always stayed in stressful situations for way too long.

I don't want to do it anymore. My wellness is worth something, and I no longer want to sacrifice it to serve others. I know I can help in ways that don't hurt me in the process. If it's causing me harm, then I am not bringing my best self forward.

My patients deserve someone who's fully committed, and the truth is, I am not. I am aching inside with the tension of being unaligned. Constantly bombarded with energy I do not want to receive.

It's okay to release this job.

Every day, I stare death in the face and am compelled to see the sacredness of life. And then I see my life and feel like it's a movie on repeat. I am in survival mode because of a job... again.

I worked so hard to get away from a stressed life. And here I am, back at it, wreaking havoc on my nervous system. I work so hard to be calm, but the circumstances remain the same.

It's time to make some big fucking changes.

June 20, 2023
Discipline

Discipline is doing things you don't want to do right now, for the greater good of your life. Annoying today, beneficial results tomorrow. I've been on a journey to embrace discipline for the past two years. It is difficult for someone who generally feels uncomfortable just existing, to lean into things that will make them feel more uncomfortable. But here we are, and from what I've learned it's how we grow.

Quitting my job today took discipline and courage. I walked into the office and did the hard task first. Running away and avoiding seemed like a much better option, but that would mean continuing to work for this dysfunctional system. I knew that was not what was in my best interest, so I embraced the discomfort. Discomfort around disappointing others is something I will have to keep walking into for the next five weeks. I know I can do it, and by the end of it all those feelings will just be memories, and I will be free.

I also didn't feel like writing tonight. I'm tired, but I made a commitment to chronicle this journey for the next lunar cycle. So, I did the thing, even if I didn't really want to tonight. Discipline.

I'm still in the seed planting phase of the new moon. My watch says: *I see a bright future ahead.*

Yes, Universe. I do too. Thank you.

Guidance from ChristiBella

Be disciplined, do the right things even when they're hard.
With aligned action, your future will be
what you dream it to be.

June 21, 2023

Coping

I got lost in replaying my workday. The pain of the past, pressing into my present. I keep seeing, feeling, and reliving these experiences. There is no benefit in watching the reels play out in a repetitive loop. I need to make a shift. Here are my intentions:

I breathe out and release the energy I absorbed that does not serve me. I release it from my mind, body, soul, cells, DNA, vibration and every aspect of my being.
I release, I release, I release.

I breathe in and embrace peace, calm, harmony, Love. I embrace these energies in my mind, body, soul, cells, DNA, vibration, and every aspect of my being.
I embrace, I embrace, I embrace.
Thank you, Spirit, for this healing.

I need to remember the things I enjoy doing and that make me feel better. Having a list can help me when I'm not sure what to do to cope.

. . .

Self Care List:

- Reiki
- RHEI
- Crystals
- Singing Bowls
- Journaling
- Yoga
- Hikes
- Water
- Music
- Dancing
- Laughing
- Creating
- Connecting
- Channeling
- Deep Breathing
- Exercising
- Affirmations
- Reading
- Baths
- Meditation
- Getting dressed up

As I just made the list, I am reminded of how many things I can do, for free, that help me heal. Simple practices of self care and self love that raise my vibration and bring me back to alignment with my authentic self.

Energy is free, intention is free, movement is free, nature is free, channeling is free, laughing and dancing are free. Self care does not have to be expensive. However, if there are things you like to indulge in sometimes, I say go for it. My boyfriend and I love a good book haul trip. It's not something we do all the time, but when we do, it lights us up.

Make a self care list for yourself. Come back to it when you need to shift your vibration away from the dark and heavy to the light and free. And if there's any resistance to taking time for you, work with those parts, uncover the beliefs, and RHEI the heck out of them! You deserve the Love and care you give so freely to others. I do too.

June 22, 2023

Creative Freedom

I did a Guided Imagery and Music (GIM) session with Meredith today. Meredith is the music therapist for the hospice company I work for. She is a beautiful soul whose presence alone is very healing.

GIM is an incredible music therapy modality where you go on a classical musical journey while in a meditative state. The therapist will have you reflect on your experience to help you uncover what your system is processing through the music and deepen the healing.

I could feel the music moving through my body and saw waves and swirls of energy in my mind's eye. It helped me move a lot of stuck energy. The internal guidance I received is that my system wants a simpler life. Less stuff, responsibilities, and energetic clutter. To clear the space and create a more intentional existence.

Other guidance I received during the session is that I want, and need, to write more. I will start devoting more time to it soon. When my only job is to create content, I will make sure I give myself time to write. I will match action with intention, to cultivate the energy of writing and creating as my profession.

I can see the life I want. A life of creative freedom, time in nature, time to move my body, and expand my mind. I want to help others live a life that feels aligned for them too.

Brittany Rose

It is a vision I know I can create. I have the Universe on my side. My heart is pure, and I am here to help others and heal me too.

I am almost there. Hang on sister, life's about to get a lot better.

June 23, 2023

I needed a day.

I gave myself the day off and I don't even feel bad about it. My stomach felt like I was being stabbed from the inside out when I woke up this morning. Thankfully, that pain has receded, but I also need and deserve some time to myself. It's time to rest and to go within. And finally... allow myself time to escape into another world.

Our society promotes self care but does not always truly support it. This company doesn't even pretend to promote self care. It is a work-all-day-and-night job for many people. Which I get, since it's literally dealing with life and death. However, I am not a medical professional, and I cannot allow it to be that way for me. I need to have balance, peace, and calm. I need time and space to process and nurture me so that on Monday I can fully show up for them.

Heaviness wraps around my heart. I need to release the guilt I feel about choosing me. Leaping towards myself means leaving behind vulnerable people. To parts of me it feels so selfish to pursue my goals and dreams.

Your hopes and dreams are what will bring light into the world, Dear One. There will always be other people who will work for hospice, because it is more aligned with their soul path. This is no longer aligned with yours. It was for a while, but now we are guiding you that it's time to move on. It is time to write, to create, express. You already know struggle, now it is time to rise from it. Do not feel guilty. Focus on all that you have already given. Your time was a gift, but you are not beholden to keep on giving to this cause. You are allowed to shift course. It is time to bloom into your authentic self, and show others how they can do that too. Love, ChristiBella

I can feel the truth in these words from my spirit, the wisest part of my being. If I am in the energy of Love and joy, I will radiate that outward, positively affecting others I encounter. This is how we ALL can spread more Love and light, do things that cause us to live in that vibration!

Reading is something I love to do but has been so difficult for me this year. As anxious as I've been, my brain hasn't been quiet enough to let me read for pure enjoyment. It feels like something got broken, and with this inability to focus, my mind is a wandering mess.

I have to retrain myself to read again. Quieting my mind through meditation and forcing myself to read are the only ways I'm going to get back into the habit.

I'm proud of myself. I read the first chapter of *A Court of Mist and Fury*, by Sarah J Maas, and a few pages of *Living with Joy* by Sanaya Roman. It feels good to hold a book in my hands and be able to focus for a few minutes. I plan on reading more again later.

. . .

I feel like it's necessary to do some prep work before I hurl myself off the cliff to reach the land of self-employment. There are many things that could block my success. I need to focus on healing these limiting beliefs and unaligned energies so that I can create a helpful, successful, abundant healing platform. I'm going to write out all the limiting beliefs my parts are holding onto that I can access right now.

Limiting Beliefs:
    I am not good enough.
    I am not smart enough.
    Being rich isn't for me.
    It's too complicated to be successful.
    People are better than me.
    It's not realistic to think I could be successful.
    I'm not worthy.
    I'll never be successful.
    I'm never going to be financially stable.
    I'll never be happy.
    I am doomed to hate my work.
    People don't make a living the way I want to.

As I wrote those words, I felt nauseous. Lurking fears lodged in my core, planted there by past versions of me. I do not have to continue to own these ideas and claim their energy. I can let them go.

I set the intention and release this energy from my mind, body, spirit, cells, DNA, vibration, and every aspect of my being. Please take this energy and transmute back into pure Love and light.

I Embrace:
    I am good enough.
    I am intelligent.

Brittany Rose

I am intuitive.
I am magnet for abundance.
I am capable.
I can do hard things.
My best is good enough.
I am living out my wildest dreams.
I am very successful.
I attract wealth.
I am filled with joy.
I am happy with the work I do.
I am a lightworker, what I create helps the world.
I am aligned with my soul in all aspects of life.

*I embrace these intentions into my mind, body, soul, cells,
DNA, vibration, and every aspect of my being.*

June 24, 2023

Unwanted Manifestations

Well. My negativity chickens have come home to roost. Stress has manifested an unfortunate circumstance into my life.

I have a suspended driver's license. I cannot drive. This job depends on my ability to drive. I have four more weeks left. I have no clue how long this is going to take to fix. What the hell am I going to do?

My energy has been so anxious and frustrated. When that's my predominant vibration, the Universe has no choice but to give me more of that. This is terrible, I am fighting off panic. Breathe, Brittany, just breathe.

What needs to happen is a shift in my vibration. The best way I know how to right now is through Reiki and gratitude. I place a hand on my chest and call in Reiki Love and light. I feel the energy flow into me, working throughout my mind and body. Tension rolls out of me, and I breathe a little deeper. As I allow the energy to flow into me, I call in thoughts of gratitude.

I am very grateful for:

1. Jonathan's Love and support

2. Money available to me.
3. A house to live in.
4. Parents who support me.
5. Food to eat.
6. Phone for all my needs.
7. A computer to do things with.
8. Books to entertain me.
9. Journals and pens to capture my thoughts.
10. My connection to Spirit.
11. The creative flow of energy.
12. My health.
13. Being in a healthy relationship.
14. Reiki.
15. Experiences, lessons, and opportunities for growth.

Thank you, Spirit, for all my blessings. I ask that you send Love and light to this situation, for the best resolution for all.
Please help align me with the highest and best outcome.
Thank you.

June 25, 2026

Healing Trust

You are allowed to be a work in progress.
Drop the need for perfectionism,
and just make one decision at a time.
Some days are more aligned than others.
You always have the choice.
Your anxiety is saying, 'we have to fear the unknown.'
It is not trusting the Universe to support you.
Why is that trust broken?
Lack of Trust=Vibration and Vibration=Reality.
If you want a different experience,
it's time to open your heart to us again.
Heal your trust issues, conquer your fears
and live the life of your dreams.
Love,
ChristiBella

I went into the Akashic Records today to work on healing my trust issues with Spirit. Although I will not fully go into why they exist, suffice it to say, my guides misdirected me for the purpose of being led to exactly where I am. But the misdirection was so big, I developed an immense wall of doubt that has made me feel disconnected from my spiritual self.

Right before I went to do this healing, my intuition guided me to a stone I have in my collection that has the word "trust" etched into it. I knew it was a sign I was on the right path with my intentions for this healing. It's time to heal and allow myself to feel safe enough to open back up. I haven't seen this stone in months, but I knew exactly where to go to find it. I also held a piece of malachite, and a piece of quartz.

When I was in the records for the healing, I saw myself in a room and there was black smoke coming out of a bowl. The smoke represented my fears and blocks to my intuition and connection with my spiritual team. Holy Fire energy was called into the bowl to help transmute the energy and release the blocks from my system.

I feel proud of myself for coming back to my spiritual practices and healing. I've been more mindful about clearing energy again with palo santo. After smudging myself and the house, I feel a lightness in the surrounding energy. I have shifted to a higher, more aligned vibration.

My watch says: *I am confident in my ability to change my life.* In other words, I trust myself and the Universe!

I am so grateful for:

- Jonathan and my supportive family.
- Health, wealth, house, food, books.
- Strength in my mind and body.
- Messages from the Universe.

June 26, 2023

The Lessons

When there is resistance, look for the lesson. I've been feeling a lot of resistance today. It is showing me what I have created with fear.

A difficult two weeks lie ahead of me at work. I will have to rely on others and learn to go with the flow instead of being in control. Getting around will not be easy, but I can do hard things.

I pulled cards and got one that says *A time to give rather than take.* Which is funny, because I'm entering a time where I have to take from others. I hate the thought of being a burden. But again, maybe here lies the lesson. I resist asking for help, but I am thrown into a situation where I must depend on others to help me.

No one can get through life alone. I am no different. I have given to others my entire life. It's okay to let others give back to me. If I keep saying it, maybe before this is over I'll believe it.

After saying some prayers and setting aligned intentions, I opened myself up for guidance. I saw something attached to my energy field. Far too often, I say, *I am a gremlin,* when I am in a bad mood. There was a little dark creature hanging out in my energy field, on my back. I got the sense that it has been contributing to the chaos in my life. Through intention and Reiki, I removed the creature from my aura, enclosed it in a container, and sent it back to the Universe.

Brittany Rose

The lesson? Be careful with your words, they create your reality. Literally. So, these are my words now:

I embrace an easy, smooth, calm, peaceful life.
I am filled with happiness, joy, Love, and creativity.
I move through life with freedom, discipline, and resilience.
I am living the life I want to live.

Sometimes, when you have a problem that you cannot immediately solve, it is best to distract yourself. I like to engage my mind or body in an activity that will help shift my focus and ultimately raise my vibration. Today, my mental health is being saved by escaping to a fantasy world, where their troubles are much more dramatic than mine.

June 27, 2023

Refocusing

People keep telling me to just quit. They say that I don't have to stick it out for the full five weeks' notice. So why don't I? Integrity and guilt. I promised I would never leave a job without full notice unless I am being abused. I am not being abused, but this job is really getting to me. There's constant drama, people not doing what they say they'll do, and our patient's care is falling through the cracks of a fractured system.

And then there is the part of me that keeps saying "it's really not that bad." Which makes me think if I shift my attention, the situation I am in with work won't feel so heavy. I need to be more in the moment with my patients. Instead of focusing on the stress, I can notice the support I bring by my presence and try to hold on to the special moments of connection.

As I write this plan, attempting to shift, I also notice a part that is scared and wants to be heard. This part feels overwhelmed by the job duties, the dynamics of the organization, and stress of hospice work in general. She just wants people to recognize what this is like for her. Some people can see my experiences, but what they offer isn't exactly helpful. Their discomfort with my pain leads to quick suggestions—eliminate the problem by just quitting. This is something I am highly unlikely to do. They want to fix it— I just want someone to hold space and see me.

So, I have to do that for myself. I can't depend on anyone else to show up for me how I want them to. They're showing up in the way they know how. This part is looking for something very specific, so it's my responsibility to give my part what it needs.

And that's what I just did. I envisioned holding her, sharing my Love with her, and reassuring her she is strong. The difficult things are temporary and won't last much longer. After sharing energy, she feels a lot better. Everything doesn't feel so heavy.

In these instances, when your system has a need and the people in your life cannot support you the way you want them to, then it is up to you to give yourself the Love that you seek. Part of my work is to find the balance between connection and independence. I need others in my life, but their presence must be without expectations... just boundaries. I don't expect you to support me, and if you cannot, then I withdraw so that I can support myself.

June 28, 2023

Shame Release

Not only am I struggling with my mental health, but I am shaming myself for that struggle. A part of me keeps saying "we did this work already, why are we back here?"

New situations, similar results. Chaos systems are disrupting my life, and I have failed to hold my center.

That Imagine Dragons song just popped into my head... *It's okay to be not okay. It's just fine to be out of your mind.*

Part of me knows it's okay—that the struggle is understandable. And then another part thinks I should be beyond this lesson. That I should have grown and become a calmer person by now.

The system has been blinking red all year, and I am tired. I believe that there's a reason for everything. If this is a test, I think the only thing I passed was leaving before the stress negatively impacted me too much. I learned I am not best suited to working in turbulent dynamics. I need work and environments that keep my nervous system regulated, where I feel free, and can create what is in my heart.

I need to forgive myself for letting stress consume me for the past six months, and honor myself for digging out of this darkness.

Spirit, please help me understand the lesson and purpose of my struggles.
Please help me release shame from my mind, body, soul, cells, DNA,
vibration, and every aspect of my being. I embrace love, compassion, peace,
and forgiveness. I am open to your guidance.

Later On...

Help came today in the form of a little preacher man. Our wonderful chaplain helped me not only with a ride around town for work, but he helped me with healing this shame.

He let me know I didn't fail hospice. I know God was speaking through him, because I never once said out loud that I felt like a failure, but it is what I've felt in my heart. Through our conversation, he helped me to see that I have actually learned a lot more about myself. I can see that I will probably never be happy working for other people and within systems. I care deeply about others, and it is an assault to my soul to see anyone, especially the vulnerable, mistreated.

Part of my guilt is that these people are the ones most in need of a voice. But he reminded me that there will always be another social worker around to help and be that advocate. I will continue to help, just in ways that are more aligned with me.

Hospice was a good experience for me, but I knew from the start it was not my forever job. It requires someone who thrives in chaos, and I am not that person. I am a person who thrives in peace. In quiet. In creativity.

Thank you, Spirit, for helping me to heal this shame.

June 29, 2023

I'm coming back.

It's amazing how much calmer I feel. A shift in perspectives yesterday has helped tremendously. My happier, more optimistic self is present today. I've done work to heal my beliefs that I failed. I have been filling my mind with more positive thoughts. Reiki is becoming a daily practice again, along with connecting with Spirit. My mind is more at ease. I know I am making the right choice by leaving this job.

Getting back to my emotional and spiritual practices is working. I'm on the path to alignment.

June 30, 2023

Fuck it.

I feel so much better than before. I have a new "fuck it" attitude. $50 in Uber fees to get around at work today? Fuck it. Ridiculousness with coworkers? Fuck it. My pants are tight? Fuck it.

I say *fuck it* in truly a non-negative way. I'm allowing life to unfold and go with the flow, even if it's not where I want it to go. Opening my mind up I look for all the lessons and opportunities for growth in this present reality. Striving to embrace the practice of radical acceptance. I do it best with diffusion, a little 'fuck it' if you will.

Actually, I'm getting excited about life again. Eagerness fills me, screaming out the desire to work on my goals and manifest my dreams. That time is coming—I can see it, I can feel it, and I know it will be magnificent.

Spirit has been speaking to me through various messengers. I continue to get the confirmation that I can make my vision a reality. I must lean into these thoughts, feelings, and messages and do manifestation practices to reinforce the energy.

I claim:
A happy, healthy, harmonious life.
A life filled with abundance, joy and freedom.

I work in alignment with my highest good and the highest good of all.
I give my heart and channel Love in all my words and deeds.
I am aligned with the highest frequencies of Love, Light, Consciousness
I am safe. I am secure.
I am the creator of my very best reality.
I am fulfilled and feel content in my heart.
I make a positive impact in the world.
The way I serve heals me too.
I love my life and am so grateful for all my blessings.
I am open to Love and share it freely.

July 1, 2023
The Light & Darkness

I have tried to live in the light for so long—I forgot there was any spiritual darkness. Last night reminded me that what you give energy to, you call into your existence.

We have been watching a documentary series, Hellier. I cannot succinctly describe this series. It starts with a paranormal investigative team looking for goblins in Kentucky and ends with them performing a ritual for the Greek deity, Pan. But there were all kinds of synchronicities and unexplained phenomena throughout the years this team has investigated this area of Kentucky.

Last night, Jonathan was out playing Magic: The Gathering, and I went to the bathroom and the light was on. I distinctly remembered the last time I went to the bathroom I turned the light off. I chalked it up to faulty memory. I decided to leave the light on and see what would happen. A few minutes later I came back to the bathroom, and the light was off.

I went back to the living room, sat down, and felt a coldness on my face. Then, something touched the back of my neck. Even though I spent my entire adolescence experiencing paranormal activity, it freaked me out. No wonder my nervous system is so easily thrown out of whack — I spent my adolescence scared of the house I lived in.

This time, however, I remembered the spiritual support I have available to me that I didn't know about back then. I called in Archangel Michael, the protector. I asked him to encase me and and the house in light to keep us safe.

I did Reiki and smudged the house with Palo Santo. I set intention for only the highest vibrational energy allowed inside our home. To reinforce, I did those same steps again today, too.

I don't think it was malevolent. Just some invisible entity trying to get my attention. Well, they succeeded.

It's another reminder: be careful of your vibration. The media you consume influences your energy. Your frequency=your experiences.

Completely Unrelated...

Got a problem? Yo, Louise will solve it.

Every physical ailment I encounter I turn to the Louise Hay book, *You Can Heal Your Life*. Lately, I have been experiencing a little tooth pain. The mental energy that causes tooth pain is indecision.

I have difficulty making decisions. I defer to others, to be agreeable and easygoing. It takes the pressure off me to make the right choice. But that's no way to live. I also get frustrated with myself because sometimes I just really don't know what I want. I look inside for an answer and all I hear are crickets.

The affirmation from the book made my mouth tingle. I can usually feel the words shifting energy in me. I also want to write some of my own.

I can make decisions with ease.
I can hear my intuition clearly.
I am spiritually guided.
I make all my decisions in alignment with the highest good of all.
I trust myself to make aligned decisions.
I am allowed to decide for myself.

July 2, 2023

My Value

Today I healed through movement. Walking, stretching, exercising, cleaning, and preparing for the week ahead.

My body feels more open. Stronger in my frame than before. I am figuring out the dance of alignment between my mind and body. It's very easy for me to walk too far to one side or the other, neglecting my body for my mind or my mind for my body.

I even allowed myself some time to read for pleasure. It is an activity that I enjoy so much, but that I always put last. It serves no other purpose than to entertain me.

But stories speak in universal truths. We get to the heart of humanity by hearing the tales of others. If that's not critical to being a helper on this planet, then I do not know what is.

However, do I really need a justification to allow time and space to entertain myself? To do something for no other reason than it's what I want? Why is that so hard for me? And so easy for me to tell others to do it?

I exist in the realm of double standards. A reflection of a part still not believing my value. It holds on to the idea that my value comes from being of service to others. And since reading is for my pleasure, it is an act of selfishness.

Thank you for revealing yourself, Service Part. I invite you to release this belief. I am allowed and deserving of relaxing and enjoyable life.

After I did a healing with this part of self, ChristiBella told me that there's a difference between being selfish and self led. Self led is when your authentic being guides you, being selfish is direction from your ego. Self led takes care of self, and when possible, supports others. Being selfish is when your focus is only your wants and does not consider anyone else.

Therefore, it's okay to be self led, and to just read a book!

July 3, 2023

Open to Love

In meditation I asked how to align with my highest good. The answer was no surprise—align with Love. My guides encouraged me to open my heart back up to Love. Be ready to receive it. This can be done with intentions.

Universe, fill me with Love.
Open my heart to Love.
Allow me to receive Love.
I am open to being a divine channel of Love.

My guides showed me how to channel Love instead of fear. It will take conscious work, but with awareness there is power. The more mindful I grow, the more I can set purposeful intentions, and emanate the energy of Love.

July 4, 2023

Joyful Freedom

Joy and freedom are inter-connected for me. On a day dedicated to celebrating our nation's freedom, I am allowed to spend my time how I want. So, with my sovereign right of choice, I choose health, happiness, and joy. Jonathan and I went for a hike in the woods this morning, then to the bookstore leaving with many treasures. After, we watched the incredible new Spider Man movie, and had a lovely meal together.

These are the days my soul craves. Simple pleasures and time to connect with my best friend. Experiences that elevate my vibration and leave a smile on my face, rather than drain me.

I know another way to raise myself and heal is to continue to focus on my spiritual connection. I want to spend more time in the Akashic Records. When I retire from hospice, I will add it into my daily routine. For now, I can still spend a few minutes each day aligning my energy and receiving messages and healings.

Guided by Love. Fueled by Love. In service of Love.
You are magical, and you are frightened. That fear blocks
your light from fully coming through.
Release the fear, remove the block.

and shine your wild light blind.
You are a bright star of healing. A beacon of Love and hope.
It starts with the one and expands to all the others.
Love all as yourself, for you and all are the same.
All from the same source; and are only
different configurations of multidimensional energy.
Don't let complexity fool you, because it all
comes back to one thing...
Love.
Be aligned with Love, and you will
always know where to go.
In the light of Love you will always be able to
follow the guidance and you will know peace.
Love and Light,
ChristiBella

After channeling the message from ChristiBella, I went inside and did a healing. I found a part of me that likes to hide in the shadows—she does not want anyone to see her. She didn't want to be found, but when ChristiBella shined a spiritual light on her, she eventually relaxed and opened to receiving healing energy. She released the blocks of fear she had been holding onto and merged with my source light.

Love is the best pathway to healing. The energy ChristiBella shares with my parts is that of Love. Once they feel it, they want to be absorbed by it. Fear is what they know, Love is what they need.

So here on this day of independence, I have created within my system the freedom to be seen and the joy of being in the energy of Love.

July 5, 2023

What fills you up?

If you're not living a life that fills you up, then what are you even doing? Why did we all agree that life is suffering, and we all have to work ourselves to death?

I know that not every day will be magically carefree, but shouldn't more than a few here and there be? Shouldn't we live for every day and not just the weekend? That's how I want to live from now on—joyously and creatively free.

I release the chains of stress and anxiety from my
mind, body and soul.
I open myself to the heart of God and to a creative and peaceful life.
I embrace it, and I am ready!

My quest is to find the things that fill me up and walk towards those things. I know a few already. I know reading, writing, creating, and being in nature fill me up. Interesting conversations and adventures with my partner also light a fire in my soul. When the light sparks in the middle of an action, it is a sign from the Universe to keep going, allow yourself the freedom of enjoyment.

That's what I've been trying to do. To tune inwards and notice how things people and places feel. Light, airy, peaceful, and excited are feelings I want to move toward more often. If it feels dense and heavy, then it is unaligned for me.

July 6, 2023

Who the Hell am I?

There are moments when it feels so unclear who I am. How did I let myself get so lost?

I fell in Love.

I fell in Love and put major parts of myself aside to make room for another. He never asked this of me—I made all those choices on my own. I matched him, instead of staying centered in my being. Even in our physical world, everywhere I look is his stuff. My things have a small room shoved in the back of the house or is just laying out without a place to be.

I feel out of touch with myself. Which means I need to go inside and connect with the most authentic part of me.

You know the first step; ask to connect with me. Ask to hear my voice and understand my guidance. You are always you, but you get to choose which side comes through. All souls are filled with both light and dark. We can help the dark, but to do that it needs to meet the light.

You know the power of connecting parts. This is something you need to do daily. This is a practice of healing

fear with Love.
Meet your parts, greet and accept them,
and then shower them with my energy.
I was never far away from you. A part showed up to protect
you, even from me. Now that you see it, you can heal it. You
can release the blocks to our connection.
Heal the fear and embrace Love!
ChristiBella

I did the healing guided by ChristiBella, and now I feel the bliss of union with my authentic self again.

July 7, 2023

Core Values

My values are at odds with my actions. Integrity is eating away at me. That voice that says work harder, help more. Be fully present until the very end. But it's countered with sheer exhaustion. A part of me wants to take it easy because I am so tired. It says—what are they going to do, fire me?

At my core, that isn't who I am. I care about people. This isn't a widget making job—this work is actual life and death.

In the end, I compromised with my parts. Today I'll take it a little easier, and Monday I get back to work. I will do the job to the best of my ability while I am still there.

I am aware that I struggle with balancing multiple priorities. I can do really well in one area of my life and fall flat in another. This is something I really need to figure out for myself.

How do others have harmony in all aspects of life? Are there people who can master it all? Healthy mind, body, and soul? Who out there can balance their responsibilities with play effectively? That's the life I am seeking. Supporting all areas of my wellness, work hard and play even more.

I guess when you examine it, you can see some of my values reflected in these desires and choices. I do value hard work, but also equally value self-care. It's just a little harder to convince myself to engage in self-care than it is in the hard work.

Which leads us right back to... self worth.

In this moment it is clear once again that I value giving to others more than I value giving to myself. To all of my parts, I deserve to be cared for too. I am allowed to rest. I am allowed to fill up my well. I am allowed to honor my needs just as much, if not more, than I honor the needs of others.

We've got some belief clearing work to do here.

July 8, 2023

Healing Billy

The Michael Franti concert was the experience my soul needed. His music, presence is so uplifting. It was a beautiful night of joy, love, laughter, and fun.

Thank you, Universe, for the magical evening! I want to keep these happy feelings with me for as long as possible.

However, it's a new day and time for new healing. I need to figure out why I've been overeating again. It has been getting worse and I am afraid to check the scale. So instead of shaming myself, I am taking control and going to change this. But I really need the part of me that is eating excessively to come forward and talk to me.

In my mind's eye, I see a small blond-haired boy with no shirt or shoes. He has dirt covered hands and smears on his face—Billy.

Billy is afraid of when he will get his next meal. He died from starvation during one of my lives. When he's activated and there's food available, he gorges himself in case he doesn't get to eat again for a while.

I reach towards this alternative life of mine and extend love and comfort. *Billy, I need you to know this is a different lifetime. We have resources and options, and we will always have food available.*

Billy agreed he could trust me and now believes we have food whenever we want or need it. ChristiBella helped collect all the Billy fragments together that have been influencing me during this lifetime. These pieces of that lifetime gathered and grew into an adult male. He rose with my spiritual self up into the sky to disappear into another level of consciousness.

Thank you, Billy and ChristiBella for this healing. I can feel the shift inside of me. I may have more eating disordered parts, but I know the work I did today will be extremely beneficial.

July 9, 2023

Rebuild

I am feeling overwhelmed by building a business from scratch. I guess it's not exactly from scratch... I am constructing from experience.

It doesn't all have to get done at once. Even though I know this, there's a part shouting, "Go! Run! Do it all! Get it all done!"

None of that is super helpful, guys, just saying. I need calm, gentle direction. I need to feel secure in the knowledge that I have resources available.

Anxious part that is pushing so hard, thank you. It is okay to relax, to let me rest. We have time and will be okay. I can recuperate. I will learn what I need to in time. But today, I need to prepare for the week ahead.

I give myself permission to rest, to read, to watch what I want. I am allowed to take time and just enjoy myself.

I did RHEI on my beliefs around rest and self-care and also finding harmony with rest and action. I feel more settled, stable, and whole now. My soul is eager to both rest and create!

This is how I rebuild and create my most aligned life. I nurture myself, and fill my well back up, so that I can channel that energy into spiritual creations.

You are opening back up to what you were born to do,
Developing programs and healings
for yourself and others.
You will need more time in quiet contemplation
when you are done with your job.
To go get more open and used to channeling
our messages again.
Archangel Michael, Archangel Metatron and
ChristiBella are here for you.
We love you and know the beautiful light
that's inside of you.
Be at peace and know all is well.
Follow the path of healing and creation, and you will
manifest your desires and dreams.
To create more stability, you need to be at ease and at peace.
Breathe and be more mindfully present.
Move and do your energy work.
Eat right and meditate often.
Think positively and create your heart song.
Love,
Your Spiritual Support Team

July 10, 2023

Deeper Layers of Healing

Earlier today I asked what parts were still over-indulgent with food. I saw in my mind's eye a squirrel stocking up, hoarding food in its mouth. Why? Because of the perceived threat of intermittent fasting. It triggers a part of me that worries there will not be enough food.

The squirrel met ChristiBella and immediately felt comforted by her. She leapt into her arms and fell asleep. She agreed to be healed by Reiki energy and when she was done, she transformed into a rabbit. I felt the energy of "eating rabbit food," meaning eating more fruits and veggies and whole natural foods.

A deeper layer of Billy also emerged while I was in meditation. It was a part of his energy that didn't integrate last time. Billy hates to feel hungry, because to him it means dying. In the eyes of a starving child, being hungry is dangerous.

I cradled Billy and reminded him that this was not his lifetime. I would always have food available to me. This part of Billy released, healed, and integrated back into my soul.

These were powerful healings for me. My eating is much better today. I walked for an hour and did 35 minutes of DDPY. I need to drink more water, but I haven't had any energy drinks today, so that's a win.

Brittany Rose

It's later in the evening and I am proud to report that I didn't snack today. No toxic chemicals consumed. I moved a lot. I'm working hard to move towards my healthiest self!

Stress and restriction create a sense of lack in my system, which activates food insecurity. Parts then want to hoard food as protection against famine. I need to let my parts know that when I forgo eating something I am making the choice for my health, not because there is scarcity.

I am hoping I released much of that and transformed today. I am very grateful for this healing. Even though I was just here a few days ago, this time I got to an even deeper layer.

July 11, 2023

Missing my Zest

I've lost so much of my zest and passion for life. Last year, my focus was on DDPY and writing. I had my business and Grandma to care for, but I had so much more time to focus on those things than I have this year.

Now, I am spread thinner. The things I am excited about and give me a sense of purpose, I don't have enough energy for. I am depleted and craving rest. Mentally and emotionally, I am drained, so I feel like I only have time to give to my passions on the weekends.

I did an hour of walking and a 15-minute DDPY today, which is definitely not my best effort. But... It was some movement. I could have done nothing, but at least I did something. It's better than where I was three years ago.

I just need to prioritize writing and stillness for the rest of tonight. Soon I will give more energy to my passions. I'll have time to figure things out.

Thank you, God, for the ability to quit my job and start my career over (again). I am ready to manifest my life to the next level. I am ready to co-create my wildest dreams.

I am a self-employed creative entrepreneur making a very abundant living as a content creator. I love what I do and am so happy with every

aspect of my life. We live in a beautiful home that has a ton of open and storage space. We can travel and do fun things. I am very healthy and active, fit, flexible and strong. I love my life. Only good things come my way. My work does good for me and good for others. I am living my happiest, healthiest, most harmonious life.
Thank you, thank you, thank you.
As I write and speak these intentions, I create alignment for my highest good and the highest good of all.

Blocks popped up as I was visualizing my ideal life. I looked inside to see what they were. The first block appeared as a curtain and opened to show me three different paths. Two not so great, but the one straight ahead was a life of success and happiness. My guides asked me if I was ready, I said yes.

Other blocks revealed themselves. Fears of not being good enough, of failing, of not having enough, shared their tales and then ChristiBella provided Love and comfort. Each released, healed, transformed, and integrated with my energy.

I must continue to feel into the blocks. I can tell inside of me what resistance feels like, it's tension in my core. When I feel that, that is the time to go inwards, explore and figure out where healing needs to occur.

I am moving forward with renewed optimism and positivity. If I dream it, believe it, and do it, I can create it.

July 12, 2023

Doing the Best I Can

The macro nutritional puzzle is something I have been trying to figure out. I am not sure I am equipped to do it.

Honestly, I just want to eat intuitively. I want Spirit to guide me, because math is hard and thinking about it too much disrupts my nervous system. I over analyze and then create stress in my body, which defeats the purpose of my health efforts.

I know what to cut down on: fat, salt, sugar. I've already mostly cut out gluten and dairy. Fat and salt are the hardest for me right now. I feel like eating more protein inevitably equals more fat and salt, but really, I just need to find low fat and low sodium alternatives.

I am tired. I should have written earlier.

Not every day will a flower produce a bloom. But we certainly cherish the days they do.

July 13, 2023

Creating Alignment

I have looked and searched and pondered what the right formula for weight loss could be for me. But that's not how I work best. Visualization, affirmation, and creating a healthy body from the inside out are the things that are most aligned with my soul.

My way to losing weight won't be by obsessing over macros. It will be through visualization and intuitive guidance. I am being guided back to the Gabriel Method. It helped me before and I believe it will help me again. The bonuses he offers in just one course is incredible. I am very excited to integrate the program into my life.

It's time to get healthy and fit again, body. I can release the weight again. It's time to radiate divine health and be at my optimal fitness level.

Learning and understanding the Gabriel Method will help me to help others, as well. That is always a driver for my learning—'will I be able to pass this on to others?'

How very 2-like of me (just a little enneagram humor, IYKYK). On *We Can Do Hard Things*, Suzanne Stabile said, "The healthier I get, the less I do." She's a fellow enneagram 2. To me that means, when I am a healthier version of me, I give myself permission to give to myself more than others. This is a theme I keep coming back to lately.

I'll always be a helper. That was programmed into my DNA. But I am trying to help in a less energetically draining way.

Spirit, please help me manifest these soul callings.
I want to do good for the world while honoring me. Thank you.

July 14, 2023

True to Me

I stayed aligned in my core today. When tested, I remained true to myself. My boss asked me to stay part time, and I said, NO.

NO to more stress. NO to more chaos. NO to unalignment.

I chose me.

It's time for me to leave. I'm ready to devote myself to my health and my creations. The preparations have begun, and I refuse to go back. When I am done with something, I am done with it. And the most honest truth is, I am not growing here. The stress is destroying my physical health and has prevented me from losing weight all year. Who completes 75Hard and not lose weight? That would be me.

Stress has also blocked me from dedicating myself to my writing and creative projects.

Although I am extremely grateful that I have so much energy and inspiration today. I've made a lot of progress on my website. My soul really wants to create a community again. I miss my Women's Circle days of connecting with like-minded individuals. The Growth Garden popped into my head... we'll see where it goes.

It feels so good to be back in the flow of creative energy. I love receiving downloads from Spirit. In this moment, I feel the tug of possibility, freedom, and all the meaningful connections available to me.

. . .

Tend to your soil.
Plant your seeds.
Grow your roots.
Align and Bloom.

July 15, 2023

Trusting Myself

I'm learning to trust myself, my instinct, and my intuitive guidance. The Universe tested me to sway from the path by giving me a dose of flattery. Someone offered me their guidance today on how I can lose weight. It felt amazing to have them say they believed in me and wanted to help me. There was a part of me that wanted to please my flatterer.

However, I know that being led by someone else isn't what's right for me now. I need to be led by my spirit and to go with my internal flow, rather than someone else's.

The offer was truly kind, but I am setting a boundary that is right for me. I cannot even tell you how monumental this is. Any other time in my history, I would have said yes and then gotten off my path. I said no again, twice in two days, to people wanting me to do what they want me to do. NO is my answer, because I trust myself and know my spirit will lead me to what I need to do.

I am very grateful for all the support surrounding me. I am grateful people care enough to reach out and check in and offer their guidance.

This new phase of my life has me EXCITED! When I started writing this, I was not excited about anything in life. I was a depleted shell of a person trying to claw my way to the light. But in a month of being focused on working on my mind, body, soul, I already feel I've shifted in big and powerful ways. My anxiety is so much less intense than it was.

I am not looking forward to saying goodbye to my patients and their families. However, a lesson I'm integrating (again) is it is okay for me to disappoint others and to help myself.

July 16, 2023

Changes

The changes from the last new moon to this one has been powerful and transformative. I didn't stop planting seeds all month. I kept reinforcing the vision I have for myself, with my words, actions, and visualizations. Through these practices, I have directed my energy towards the life I want to create. It has also required me to unearth the blockages preventing my new beliefs from taking root. I went through the daily process of releasing and healing unaligned beliefs and vibration to embrace the new ones that match my soul's vision.

Here I am, a month later, feeling calmer, healthier, happier, and more creative than I was. I am much more aligned with my authentic self. There will always be somewhere to grow, but I like this inspired direction.

I choose at this moment to open my heart fully to the beauty that is me. I accept myself for who I am, who I was, and who I will be. I celebrate my growth, and my alignment. I am rising again.

It's not over yet. Watch me bloom some more.

July 17, 2023

New Moon

Happiness is within reach. It was unattainable in my previous life, because I was with a partner that was out of alignment with my soul.

But now, I know my Love is my true divine counterpart. His words and actions honor me, and he respects my dreams. I receive encouragement rather than doubt. His presence helps me to be braver.

For the life I want, I definitely need to be brave.

I am proud of myself for showing up for myself daily. For writing even when it was inconvenient. For taking a hard month and still committing to my healing and growth. I have a couple more weeks before I am done with this job, but I know better times are coming for me. I just have to be patient, and while I am in the midst of the storm, continue to work on healing my parts.

Thank you, reader, for being here with me throughout this journey. For bearing witness to my soul's quest for authentic alignment. I hope my healing has helped you get in touch with your multidimensional self, to heal, and plant new seeds for aligned transformation.

Healing is possible. It is within reach for everyone. You just have to be brave enough to venture into the darkness while reaching for the light.

Brittany Rose

The new moon is here
Into the darkness I go
To plant my seeds
Transform and grow
Breaking the gloom
Reach for the light
Align and Bloom
A beautiful new life.

Acknowledgments

First of all, thank you reader, for taking a chance on my book. This is definitely a creation of Love and I'm so glad I got to share it with you. I hope there were things you found supportive and that it helps you align with your most beautiful authentic self.

Thank you to Spirit and my authentic self, ChristiBella, for being here and helping me to write this book every step of the way. My life is so much better in connection with you.

To the Love of my life, Jonathan, thank you for believing in me and supporting my dreams so thoroughly. You're the best partner and editor a girl could ask for. I wouldn't be here right now if it weren't for you. I love you and our life together, and know it's only going to get better from here!

Thank you to my friends, family and beta readers for supporting me in the development of this book. To my parents, thank you for always supporting my wildest dreams. Sister, I appreciate that I can go to you for great feedback and wisdom.

I am eternally grateful for the people who share their heart and souls with the world to help others expand. Thank you to my teachers, Meg Gilmore-Resnick, Mary Riposo, and Emily Jean Blatt, for showing me how to embrace my authenticity and reach for the light. I also have so much gratitude for my human spirit guides, the ones I know through their words and deeds, Glennon Doyle, Brené Brown, Gabby Bernstein, and Rebecca Campbell. Your vulnerability inspires me to be brave and heal out loud.

Lastly, thank you to my writing teachers, Sarra Cannon, Abbie Emmons, Jenna Moreci and Bethany Atazadeh for making helpful content, and giving me hope that I can make my dreams come true.

Notes

Resources mentioned in the text:

1.   Christina L. Ross, PhD, BCPP, "Energy Medicine: Current Status and Future Perspectives," Global Advances in Health and Medicine Volume: 8: 1-10.

2.   William Lee Rand, "What is Reiki", International Center for Reiki Training, accessed October 30, 2023, https://www.reiki.org/faqs/what-reiki.

3.   Donna Eden and David Feinstein, Energy Medicine: Balancing Your Energies for Optimal Health, Joy, and Vitality 10th Edition (TarcherPerigree, 2008) 17-22.

4.   Vincent J. Felitti, MD, FACP, Robert F. Anda, MD, MS, Dale Nordenberg, MD, David F Williamson, MS, PhD, Alison M Spitz, MS, MPH, Valerie Edwards, BA, Mary P Koss, PhD, James S. Marks, MD, MPH, "Relationship of Childhood Abuse and Household Dysfunction to Many of Leading Causes of Death in Adults: The Adverse Childhood Experiences (ACE) Study," American Journal of Preventive Medicine, no. 14 (1998): 245-258.

5.   Emily Nagoski, PhD and Amelia Nagoski, DMA, Burnout: The Secret to Unlocking the Stress Cycle (New York: Ballatine Books, 2020).

6.   Richard C. Schwartz, Internal Family Systems Therapy (New York: The Guilford Press, 1995).

7.   Sanaya Roman, Spiritual Growth: Being Your Higher Self (Tiburon: H J Kramer, Inc, 1989).

8.   Don Miguel Ruiz, The Four Agreements: A Toltec Wisdom Book (San Rafael: Amber-Allen Publishing, 1997).

9.   Chandra Shekhar Nautiyal, Puneet Singh Chauhan, Yeshwant Laxman Nene, "Medicinal Smoke Reduces Airborne Bacteria," Journal of Ethnopharmacology 114, no 3 (December 2003) 446-451.

Made in United States
North Haven, CT
11 November 2023